Communities Left Behind: Alternatives for Development

North Central Regional Center for Rural Development

Communities Left Behind:

Alternatives for Development

The Iowa State University Press / **Ames** / 1974

A COLLECTION of papers presented during a symposium (Communities Left Behind: Alternatives for Development) at South Dakota State University, Brookings, South Dakota, May 16–18, 1973; sponsored by the North Central Regional Center for Rural Development in cooperation with South Dakota State University.

Volume Editor: **Larry R. Whiting**

© 1974 The Iowa State University Press
Ames, Iowa 50010. All rights reserved

Composed and printed by
The Iowa State University Press

First Edition, 1974

Library of Congress Cataloguing in Publication Data

Main entry under title:

Communities left behind: alternatives for development.

Papers presented during a symposium at South Dakota State University, Brookings, May 16–18, 1973; sponsored by the North Central Regional Center for Rural Development, in cooperation with South Dakota State University.

Includes bibliographies.
1. Community development—United States—Congresses. 2. United States—Rural conditions—Congresses. 3. Sociology, Rural—Congresses. I. Whiting, Larry R., ed. II. North Central Regional Center for Rural Development. III. South Dakota State University.

HN90.C6C63   309.2′63′0973   74-11286
ISBN 0-8138-0345-4

CONTENTS

FOREWORD

THIS BOOK is the result of a conference developed cooperatively by the North Central Regional Center for Rural Development, South Dakota State University, and the North Central Research Strategy Committee (NCRS-3). The planning committee included A. Gordon Ball and Robert W. Crown, the Regional Center; Selby Smith, Robert Wagner, and Laurel Howe, South Dakota State University; Martin Pond, Purdue University; Jan L. Flora, Kansas State University; G. Howard Phillips, Ohio State University; and Jerry G. West, University of Missouri.

Rural development has the prospect of being implemented through various federal and state programs that are emerging, although inadequate resources are likely to delay it. Public concern about rural development arises because of the maldistribution of the costs and benefits that have accompanied both national economic growth and the advance of technology. Rapid economic growth in the post-World War I period has concentrated in large urban and industrial centers. Though nonmetropolitan areas have seen some of this general economic growth, their share is nowhere near that of existing urban and industrial areas.

Of even more severe consequence has been the maldistribution accompanying agricultural technology. Some economic groups have clearly gained from it, others have sacrificed because of it. Farmers with the capital to expand land holdings and acquire more resources reflecting advanced technology have benefitted from it; farm workers with skills unadapted to other occupations have sacrificed in real income as they were replaced by bigger machines and other capital technology.

Manufacturers of capital inputs have gained as farmers used more of the bigger machines, but retailers in country towns have paid heavy costs as their commerce and income dwindled because of smaller populations and cost economies of large-scale input distributing facilities for agriculture. To put it more broadly, the social environment of many rural communities has eroded as declining population no longer supported health, recreational, and general services. Many country towns have become scarred with crumbling dwellings, abandoned stores, and weed covered streets.

vii

Leaders of urban centers, which had become receiving stations for workers displaced from farms and country towns, were awakened somewhat suddenly by the diseconomies of city size as reflected in environmental degradation and social upheavals. These leaders also became concerned with population and employment opportunities in rural areas. Legislative action and congressional pronouncements further reflect the attempt to improve the distribution of benefits from economic and technological advance. The solutions to rural community development lie in restoring equity in the distribution of costs and benefits from national growth and technological change.

Initially, the recipe for doing so seemed to be rural industrialization. This avenue for restoring employment opportunities, improving income, and providing a more favorable social milieu is a positive possibility for many rural communities and should be pursued with zest. But a community development program focusing mainly on rural industrialization can never fully restore equity over the countryside because the majority of country towns and rural communities just do not possess the characteristics and endowments for industrial development. Economic and social well-being will continue to revolve around the surrounding farm sector and the businesses and institutions that serve the towns. How, then, can adequate family incomes and quality personal and public services be supplied and maintained in these communities? What options are open to these communities for providing favorable opportunities for their youth, for the adult sector which provides the foundation of commerce and social organization, and for older citizens with both more free time and greater needs for particular services?

The conference reported in this volume was organized to tackle these questions and problems. Its particular focus was the rural community whose needs and possibilities largely fall outside the realm of industrial development. As such, it is the counterpart of a previous conference sponsored by the North Central Regional Center for Rural Development on behalf of communities which do have the hope and endorsement for industrialization. (See *Rural Industrialization: Problems and Potentials,* Iowa State University Press, Ames, 1974.)

The conference was held at South Dakota State University, and the university contributed greatly in program development, conference organization, and facilities. Persons and communities interested in the development facets discussed in this volume are particularly indebted to Dean Duane Acker and his South Dakota State University staff.

EARL O. HEADY
Director, North Central Regional Center
for Rural Development

PREFACE

WE OFTEN DEVOTE time and attention to *describing* what happens as a commnuity decreases in population. We describe the closing of the clothing stores, hardware stores, restaurants, and finally the school. We explain that as this happens, fewer dollars flow within the community. We describe the decreased opportunity for social interaction that results when the school board and the church board no longer exist.

Sometimes we go deeper. We study declining communities to ascertain which businesses close first or what forces interact to result in church or school consolidations. We analyze in a seemingly cold and nonsympathetic way.

I believe we occasionally ignore some topics that need to be discussed and studied in a positive way. One topic is the concept of zero population growth. For example, some universities presently need to learn how to retain viability in a situation where enrollments have either leveled off or are decreasing. In such a situation, how do you develop new curricula, bring in new faculty and ideas, provide for perpetual rejuvenation of the educational process, and maintain the "good life" within (the) academe?

Similarly, many of our communities are faced with identifying proper alternatives for maintaining viability to human life in a zero population growth situation. And, with modern contraceptives and other inhibitions to human reproduction, even some larger communities may be faced with the same problem—maintaining community viability with zero growth.

This volume gives us some substantial clues and identifies some of the characteristics considered desirable to human life within communities. The need for self-esteem, and the feeling of identification and being identified within the community are discussed and accepted as very desirable characteristics. Those of us in research and educational institutions need to do more to identify specifically those characteristics that need to be present for the "good life." We need to learn the extent to which or the conditions under which they need to be present.

Social scientists, working cooperatively with persons in other disciplines, need to quantify the social costs and benefits that accrue in communities of various sizes and various characteristics. Obviously, the first step is to identify those entities, amenities, or characteristics that have cost or benefit. Self-esteem might be one such benefit. Perhaps in this book we identify it; it needs to be quantified.

Let me offer an illustration. Twenty years ago most horticultural research workers would have said that apples taste good or bad, sour or sweet. A typical experiment station director in reviewing a research project on apples would ask, "How will you quantify flavor?" Horticulturists may have said, "We can't." Today, however, we have elucidated, identified, and quantified flavor components. I would challenge the social scientist to do the same with the social or human values that may be influenced by community size or characteristics.

The economist must learn to deal with nondollar units. Whatever units are used to quantify the characteristic of human interaction, for example, must then be used by the economist to *measure* costs and benefits, or to *apply* such useful techniques as feasibility studies or input-output equations to human and social issues.

Experiment stations, historically, have spent most of their time and energy on research that helps individuals make individual decisions. We compare 0, 30, and 50 pounds of nitrogen per acre of corn, for example, and the extension service takes this information to the farmer so that he, as an individual, can make the decision on how much fertilizer to use. Increasingly, though, we have sensed the need to help groups of people make group decisions. In experiment stations we analyze population trends and convey this information via the extension service to county commissioners, school board members, and church trustees. As groups, they can make better decisions in regard to continuing certain institutions, changing them, or making investments in them. I believe that over time the experiment station and the extension service will increasingly direct their attentions and energies to learning and teaching information for group decision making.

DUANE ACKER
Dean, College of Agriculture
and Biological Sciences
South Dakota State University

Communities Left Behind: Alternatives for Development

CHAPTER ONE

QUANTITATIVE DIMENSIONS OF DECLINE AND STABILITY AMONG RURAL COMMUNITIES

CALVIN L. BEALE

OUR COUNTRY is dotted with the remains of towns that reached their zenith generations ago—some before the Revolutionary War. This is not to imply that the phenomenon of the declining community has gone unnoticed. It has been 100 years since historian Charles Jones wrote a book-length study called "The Dead Towns of Georgia." But only the present problems of the Great Plains and western Corn Belt have caused sufficient concern to produce a rational consideration of the extent and consequences of the trend and approaches to its resolution.

Communities may decline for various reasons: natural disasters, exhaustion of natural resources, loss of transportation advantages, and loss of political status, for example. But community decline, as measured by population loss, has been at a maximum only since declining manpower needs in agriculture occurred simultaneously with forces that acted to relocate and centralize many business and community functions into larger units. Since World War I we have had the paradoxical situation that the faster our national population has grown, the faster and more extensively our small communities have declined.

About 31 percent of all counties in the country declined in population during the 1930s, when national population growth was low because of low birth rates and lack of immigration. As national population growth revived in the 1940s and went even higher in the 1950s, the number of declining counties actually rose. Despite the much higher potential for growth as a result of the high birth rate of the period, 49 percent of all counties decreased in population in the 1950s

CALVIN L. BEALE is Leader, Population Studies Group, Economic Research Service, U.S. Department of Agriculture, Washington, D.C.

as a widespread exodus to the cities occurred. Furthermore, the rate of loss among the losing counties rose. In the 1930s less than a third of the losing counties declined by as much as 10 percent in the decade, but in the 1950s, over half the losers had losses of 10 percent or more. Thus, although losses occurred in many counties earlier in the century, both the extent and depth of the losses increased after the Great Depression. It is only natural that awareness and concern about the matter should emerge.

I am not suggesting that perpetual population growth is necessarily good. Our traditional romance with the growth concept has cooled. The recent Commission on Population Growth and the American Future[1] recommended that our national population growth be slowed and eventually ended and offered persuasive arguments that as a nation we would benefit from such a result. But cessation of growth is different from active decline generated by rapid and highly selective out-migration. Further, it must be recognized that every county in the entire North Central region (Illinois, Iowa, Indiana, North Dakota, South Dakota, Nebraska, Missouri, Minnesota, Wisconsin, Michigan, Ohio, Kansas) has had levels of childbirth more than sufficient to replace the parental population. The rural people of the region who are now reaching the end of the childbearing period have had 65 percent more children than are needed for parental replacement. In other words, the North Central rural population would increase by 65 percent in every quarter century under the family size levels that people chose for themselves in the 20 years after World War II. Thus, if the rural areas do not develop economic conditions that permit retention of this potential population growth, the only alternative is further migration to the cities.

In discussing population trends, both towns and counties will be considered, with focus on the North Central states, the West North Central ones in particular. Although it is fair to say that rural communities everywhere have had difficulty with population retention in modern times, different regions have by no means had identical trends.

In any review of the population commentary on the subject, one quickly and often encounters the cliché, "the dying small town." I think comprehension of the problem by professional research workers, concerned public officials, and the public in general has been hampered by the extent to which this phrase, with its sense of hopeless finality, has permeated our consciousness. Certainly there has been considerable misunderstanding in Washington over the years about the actual trends in small communities. Part of the problem is that

1. The Commission on Population Growth and the American Future was created by Congress at the request of the President and functioned from 1970 to 1972. The commission's final report was *Population and the American Future*. 186 pp. Government Printing Office, 1972.

the term "small town" has no precise meaning. One person may use it who has in mind the grain elevator, creamery, and railroad siding hamlet of his Corn Belt youth, and his listener may be a big city native to whom any place of less than 50,000 people is a small town. The distinction is critical, because small towns of different sizes have fared differently, and variations of even several hundred in average population are associated with differences in retention of population. These variations in turn are almost certainly related to the increased variety of services and employment available in communities as population exceeds typical threshold levels at which the support of particular services and businesses becomes feasible.

Of course, the stereotype of "the dying small town" has its kernel of truth—as most stereotypes have—but when used indiscriminately as a description of all or even most small places it becomes badly misleading.

POPULATION CHANGE IN TOWNS AND COUNTIES. In a cooperative project with the Economic Research Service, Glenn Fuguitt of the University of Wisconsin has compiled data on the population changes of nonmetropolitan towns. The North Central region has nearly 5,600 incorporated towns of less than 2,500 population located in nonmetropolitan counties. This is 30 percent of all incorporated places of all sizes in the entire country. Of these rural North Central towns, 49.6 percent increased in population in 1960–70 and 50.4 percent decreased. But despite a small majority of losers, the overall population in the towns increased by 4.8 percent because the gaining towns tended to grow by larger amounts than the declining towns lost (Table 1.1). Some 3.5 million people lived in rural towns of the region in 1970, and contrary to a general impression, the number had grown by about 160,000 in the previous 10 years. But an inspection of the data by size of rural place shows considerable contrast between the largest places—those of 1,000 to 2,499 population—and the smallest—those of less than 500 population. About 64 percent of the largest places had population increases, compared with just 41 percent of the group with less than 500 people.

A further look at the data for towns of less than 1,000 people, grouped by size intervals of only 100 population each, shows that the likelihood of population retention or loss is sensitive to very small differences in population size (Figure 1.1). From less than 100 people up to 800 people, each increment of 100 population reduces the probability of a town losing population. Sixty-seven percent of the incorporated towns of less than 100 population declined. With each additional 100 people, 3 or 4 percent fewer places declined. Only among places of less than 400 people were losses more common than

TABLE 1.1. Population change in nonmetropolitan rural towns, North Central Region, 1960–70[a]

Size of Town, 1960	Number of Places			Total Population		
	Total 1960	With population loss, 1960–70		1970	1960	Percentage change, 1960–70
		Number	Percentage of total			
			(%)	(thou)	(thou)	(%)
All towns under 2,500 persons	5,566	2,803	50.4	3,498.4	3,339.3	4.8
1,000–2,499	1,063	383	36.0	1,750.5	1,640.1	6.7
900–999	150	50	33.3	148.8	142.5	4.4
800–899	217	91	41.9	190.5	183.7	3.7
700–799	261	101	38.7	205.6	195.5	5.2
600–699	289	118	40.8	203.7	186.9	9.0
500–599	334	146	43.7	188.9	182.3	3.6
400–499	505	241	47.7	233.6	227.0	2.9
300–399	605	324	53.6	212.9	210.6	1.1
200–299	828	493	59.5	205.8	204.4	0.7
100–199	933	599	64.2	134.2	140.4	−4.4
Under 100	381	257	67.5	23.9	25.9	−7.7

SOURCE: U.S. Census data by Department of Rural Sociology, University of Wisconsin, and Economic Research Service, U.S. Department of Agriculture.

[a] Nonmetropolitan status as of 1963. Incorporated places only. Excludes places that were incorporated or disincorporated during the decade.

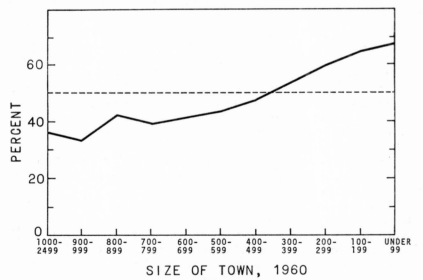

Source: Unpublished data from USDA-Univ. of Wis.,project on population change in nonmetro towns.

FIG. 1.1. Percentage of nonmetro rural towns with population loss, 1960–70, North Central region.

gains. In the 400–500 size group, 48 percent lost; from 700–800 just 39 percent lost; above that point, places of just 800–1,000 people were only a little more likely to lose population than cities of 10,000 or 25,000 people.

Places of less than 1,000 in the West North Central states had a higher probability of loss than those in the East North Central group. And among West North Central towns, declines were more numerous than gains in places with less than 500 population.

There was no increase in the 1960s in the percentage of rural-sized towns in the North Central states that lost population. The portion losing, 50.4 percent, was remarkably similar to that in the 1950s, 50.6 percent. And places of less than 500 people actually showed some reduction in incidence of loss in the 1960s. East of the Mississippi River a decentralizing trend into the nonmetropolitan countryside was evident, as open country areas shifted from a 4 percent loss of population to an 8 percent gain. Such a gain means that many of the rural towns of the East North Central division have more populous trading zone hinterlands than before. In major contrast, the open country population of the West North Central states declined by 10 percent; nearly as large a decrease as that of the 1950s (12 percent). Although there is a sense of decline in many of the West North Central towns, the more substantial loss of population has been occurring in the open country. There has been a relative drawing-in of the West North Central rural population into the towns.

Quite aside from the reality of decline in many of the small towns of the North Central region is the fact that the decline is more visible because those states have had a much greater propensity to incorporate their rural towns than have most other states. This is particularly true in the seven North Central states west of the Mississippi River (Minnesota, Iowa, Missouri, North Dakota, South Dakota, Kansas, Nebraska). In that area in 1960 there was a ratio of only 1,647 total rural people for each incorporated rural town. By contrast, the ratio of rural people to rural towns was 3,739 to 1 in the East North Central states, and 6,720 to 1 in the 12 Southern states east of the Mississippi River. In California, the extreme case, there were more than 37,000 rural people for every incorporated rural town.

Many states simply have not incorporated small towns. In such cases there is no measurement of population change available from the census and no formalized structure of local municipal government to experience decline and discouragement. The comparative lack of incorporated towns elsewhere is particularly true of places with less than 500 people. The 12 Southern states referred to have three times as many rural people as the West North Central states but less than half as many incorporated places of under 500 population. The Middle West, especially in the Plains and Western Corn Belt, has a much

TABLE 1.2. Population change of counties, 1940–70, and average initial population, North Central Region

Population Change 1940–70	North Central Region					
	Number of counties			Average 1940 population		
	Total	ENCᵃ	WNCᵇ	Total	ENC	WNC
				(thou)		
Total	1,056	437	619	38.0	60.9	21.8
Loss	547	120	427	17.0	22.4	15.5
—35.0 or more %	104	7	97	10.2	12.3	10.1
—20.0 – —34.9%	190	29	161	16.9	19.2	16.4
—10.0 – —19.9%	136	41	95	18.7	23.6	16.5
0.0 – — 9.9%	117	43	74	21.3	25.2	19.1
Gain	509	317	192	60.5	75.5	35.9
0.0 – 9.9%	101	49	52	22.9	22.4	23.3
10.0 – 19.9%	78	41	37	26.1	30.4	21.4
20.0 – 29.9%	65	42	23	35.4	40.0	27.1
30.0 – 49.9%	96	71	25	129.4	157.1	50.7
50.0 or more %	169	114	55	69.5	76.7	54.5

ᵃ East North Central Division.
ᵇ West North Central Division.

larger inventory of communities accustomed to an organized corporate life and therefore more sensitive to decline and more observable when they do decline.

There appear to be 14 counties (6 in Missouri, 5 in Kansas, and 1 each in Indiana, Nebraska, and Ohio) that have had consecutive population decline in every census since 1890, showing how long and unremitting an adjustment of population to changed circumstances can be. But the more important losses that continue to shape everyday life are probably those that have occurred since 1940. In general, they are the heaviest declines and have taken place since the end of the rather atypical period of the Great Depression.

A comparison of county population changes from 1940 to 1970—without regard to intermediate changes—shows the concentration of the heaviest losses in the West North Central division (Table 1.2 and Figure 1.2). A handful of counties have declined by more than half in 30 years. About 97 of the 619 counties in the West North Central region have lost 35 percent or more of their 1940 population, but they are not closely grouped. They include most of the Flint Hills grazing area in Kansas, the southern Sand Hills in Nebraska, the Corn Belt margin counties along the Nebraska-Kansas border and the Missouri-Iowa border, and many counties in western North Dakota. Very few of the counties with heaviest losses are east of the Mississippi River.

In general, the higher the rate of loss, the smaller the initial average county size. Those decreasing by 35 percent or more had a 1940 average population of 10,200, those with up to 10 percent loss

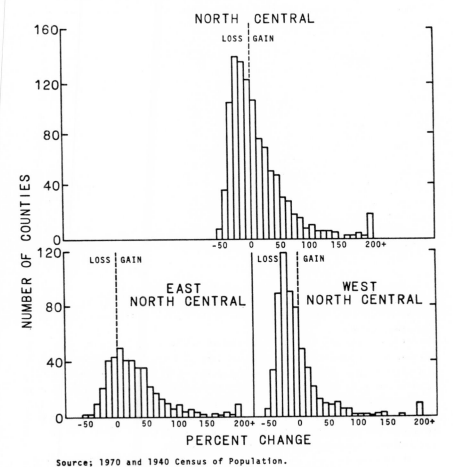

Source; 1970 and 1940 Census of Population.

FIG. 1.2. Counties by population change, 1940–70.

averaged 21,300 people initially, and those that gained by more than 50 percent averaged 69,500.

In the course of a decade, out-migration rates are highest for persons reaching age 20 during the period. In counties of most severe population loss—say where it has dropped by 20 percent in just 10 years—the net out-migration rates are often 50 percent or more for young adults. However, they are much lower for persons over 30. In less extreme cases of loss, the out-movement of young adults will be 35 to 40 percent and that of persons over 30 will be less than 10 percent. With some exceptions, the rural communities of the North Central region are not suffering from rapid out-movement of established

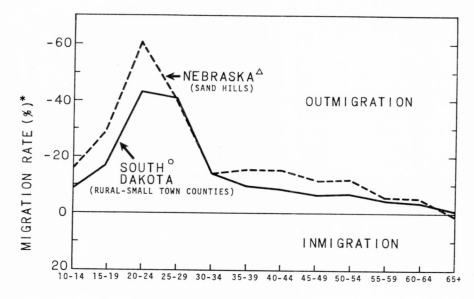

AGE IN 1970

* Change due to net migration expressed as a percentage of persons expected
  to survive to 1970.
△ 15 contiguous Sand hills counties.
○ Counties with no town of 10,000 or more people in 1960.

Source: Unpublished data from USDA-Univ. of Ga., net migration project.

*FIG. 1.3. Net migration rates by age, for selected Nebraska and
            South Dakota counties, 1960–70.*

families but from continued loss of young adults. And this loss extended over several decades leads to progressively smaller numbers of
established families and children.

The pattern of out-migration by age is illustrated in Figure 1.3.
Part of the data relates to all counties in South Dakota that did not
have a city of 10,000 or more people in 1960. These counties experienced an overall decline of 6.6 percent in population from 1960–70.
For contrast, the chart also shows migration rates for a block of 15
counties in the Nebraska Sand Hills that averaged 15.2 percent population decline in the same decade.

In the rural and small town counties of South Dakota, out-migration was nearly 15 percent for the 1960 population surviving to 1970.
It was 43 percent for those who reached age 20–24 during the decade
but less than 10 percent for all groups aged 35–39 or older.

In the Sand Hills counties, overall net out-movement was nearly
20 percent. The rate reached majority proportions among youth attaining age 20–24, where 60 percent left during the 10 years, and re-

mained above 10 percent for all age groups up through persons reaching age 50–54. In this area, it is the minority of youths who remain behind who are probably most selective in character, rather than those who leave. Active displacement of population extends to people well up into middle age, where considerable personal strain may attend a move made that late in life.

FACTORS INDUCING POPULATION LOSS. The most important factor behind the decline of population in rural areas of the North Central region has been dependence on industries with declining manpower needs—farming in particular and mining to a lesser extent. One farmer can handle a great increase in acreage with modern technology, and farmers need high volume to counteract eroding profit margins, so a major reduction in the number of farms has resulted from these forces. Mining activity has experienced the same reductions in manpower from mechanization as has farming, and in addition has had employment losses from exhaustion of deposits.

If the counties of the North Central region are grouped by degree of dependence on farm and mine employment in 1960, the association between such dependence and population retention is very clear (Table 1.3). In the region as a whole, there were 94 counties in which more than 50 percent of employed workers were in agriculture (farm production work) or mining. All but six of them decreased in population during 1960–70. There were 159 counties where 40–49 percent of all workers were in agriculture and mining, and all but 15 decreased in population. Only where farm and mine work de-

TABLE 1.3. Population change, 1960–70, of counties by percent of workers employed in agriculture and mining 1960, North Central Region

Percentage of Workers Employed in Agriculture and Mining, 1960	Number of Counties with		Population		
	Population increase 1960–70	Population decrease 1960–70	1970	1960	Percentage Change 1960–70[a]
			(thou)	(thou)	(%)
Total	526	530	56,575.0	51,617.5	9.6
50% and over	6	88	466.8	536.1	—12.9
40–49	15	144	1,578.1	1,733.4	—9.0
30–39	64	138	2,827.2	2,870.5	—1.5
20–29	105	97	4,062.8	3,953.1	2.8
Less than 20%	336	63	47,640.2	42,524.5	12.0

[a] The relationship between percentage change in population 1960–70 and percentage employed in agriculture and mining 1960 is $Y = 17.36 - .56X$ with a coefficient of determination (r^2) of .37. On the average there was a .56 percentage point decline in population change for every percentage point increment in employment in agriculture and mining.

TABLE 1.4. Change in private nonfarm wage and salary employment, 1959–69, and population, 1969–70, by rurality of counties[a]

Area and Rurality of Counties	Employment (thou)		Population (thou)		Percentage Change (%)	
	1969	1959	1970	1960	Employment 1959–69	Population 1960–70
United States	55,862.9	41,293.0	203,156.4	179,323.2	35.3	13.3
0–29.9% rural	39,712.0	29,897.8	122,899.6	106,699.2	32.8	15.2
30.0–49.9	7,194.6	5,115.2	30,221.3	26,139.0	40.7	15.6
Predominantly rural	8,956.4	6,280.0	50,035.5	46,485.0	42.6	7.6
50.0–69.9	5,586.8	3,926.4	27,193.8	24,547.3	42.3	10.8
70.0–99.9	2,391.9	1,681.6	14,649.5	13,752.1	42.2	6.5
Entirely rural	977.7	672.0	8,192.3	8,185.6	45.5	0.1
East North Central Division	12,108.3	9,251.9	40,252.5	36,225.0	30.9	11.1
0–29.9% rural	8,700.8	6,815.4	25,129.4	22,549.8	27.7	11.4
30.0–49.9	1,768.1	1,277.0	6,390.8	5,680.6	38.5	12.5
Predominantly rural	1,639.4	1,159.6	8,782.2	7,994.6	41.4	9.2
50.0–69.9	1,139.1	809.9	5,381.9	4,914.8	40.6	9.5
70.0–99.9	410.5	288.8	2,649.6	2,420.1	42.1	9.5
Entirely rural	89.9	60.9	700.7	659.7	47.7	6.2

12

TABLE 4.1. (continued)

West North Central Division, 1st tier[b]					
0–29.9% rural	3,049.3	2,252.6	11,317.2	10,491.2	35.4	7.9
30.0–49.9	2,167.7	1,612.3	5,828.2	5,269.7	34.5	10.6
Predominantly rural	286.1	198.1	1,332.3	1,140.1	44.4	16.9
50.0–69.9	595.4	442.2	4,156.7	4,081.4	34.6	1.8
70.0–99.9	312.7	232.8	1,847.8	1,784.2	34.3	3.6
Entirely rural	176.7	131.1	1,326.2	1,303.3	34.7	1.8
	106.1	78.3	982.7	994.0	35.5	−1.1
West North Central Division, 2nd tier[c]					
0–29.9% rural	1,055.7	796.2	5,013.3	4,929.9	32.6	1.7
30.0–49.9	621.2	466.3	2,127.6	1,953.0	33.2	8.9
Predominantly rural	227.5	164.4	1,104.7	1,066.7	38.3	3.6
50.0–69.9	207.0	165.5	1,781.0	1,910.2	25.1	−6.8
70.0–99.9	91.7	73.4	658.3	655.7	24.9	0.4
Entirely rural	22.1	17.1	183.1	198.2	29.0	−7.6
	93.2	74.9	939.6	1,056.3	24.4	−11.0
South Region					
0–29.9% rural	15,410.3	10,519.6	62,795.2	54,973.1	46.5	14.2
30.0–49.9	8,718.3	6,032.3	29,029.1	24,206.8	44.5	19.9
Predominantly rural	2,380.2	1,623.2	9,740.5	8,429.3	46.6	15.6
50.0–69.9	4,311.8	2,864.2	24,025.6	22,337.0	50.5	7.6
70.0–99.9	2,412.8	1,583.5	11,246.8	10,080.6	52.4	11.6
Entirely rural	1,358.6	917.0	8,202.2	7,737.7	48.1	6.0
	540.4	363.6	4,576.6	4,518.7	48.6	1.3

SOURCE: U.S. censuses of population and county business patterns.

[a] Counties grouped by percentage of population classified as rural in 1960.

[b] Iowa, Minnesota, and Missouri.

[c] Kansas, Nebraska, North Dakota, and South Dakota.

13

pendence was less than 30 percent did half of the counties avoid population loss, and only where such work was less than 20 percent of all work did growth occur in the great majority of counties. The bivariate correlation between percentage in farm and mine work and rate of population growth was $r = -61$; $r^2 = .37$.

The nature of this relationship creates very different patterns of population change between the West North Central states and the East North Central states. Nearly all counties where agricultural and mining dependence was over 40 percent were in the western half of the region. Such levels of dependence make any population growth very unlikely. New jobs in other industries can rarely be developed fast enough under such conditions to offset decline in the traditional work.

In the United States in general, the more rural counties did succeed in obtaining the highest growth rate of private nonagricultural wage and salary jobs during the 1960s. For example, the entirely or predominantly rural counties of the United States as a whole had a 43 percent increase in such jobs, compared to a growth of 34 percent in the predominantly urban counties (Table 1.4). Rural nonagricultural job growth was especially high in the South where the rural counties averaged better than 50 percent growth in these jobs in just 10 years. Nonagricultural job growth levels in the East North Central states resembled those of the United States as a whole, with the more rural areas having rapid growth. West of the Mississippi River, the average nonagricultural growth rates were lower, and the comparative advantage of higher growth in the more rural counties was absent. As a result, a county with a given level of agricultural or mining dependence was less likely to decline in the East North Central states than in the western group.

The Plains tier of states in the West North Central division has suffered not only from the heaviest dependency on extractive industries but also from the least relative success in obtaining alternative employment. These states (the Dakotas, Nebraska, and Kansas) had higher nonagricultural job growth in the predominantly urban counties rather than in the rural ones, contrary to the national pattern; and the growth rate of the rural counties was only 25 percent, compared with 41 percent east of the Mississippi River and 51 percent in the South. The Plains tier of the West North Central states has not been able to obtain significant rural job development, despite the very modest absolute increase that would be needed to produce rapid percentage gains from a small base.

Note from Table 1.4 that a 45 percent increase in private nonagricultural wage and salary jobs in the entirely rural counties of the nation resulted in only a 0.1 percent increase in population, whereas a 33 percent job gain in the most urban counties was accompanied by a 15 percent increase in population. Growth in a job sector that has one job for every twelve people—as was the case in the entirely rural counties at the beginning of the decade—simply does not have the same power to hold population as does growth in a job sector that has less than four people for each job (such as in the most urban counties).

Unlike large areas of the South, the out-movement from the small communities of the North Central region is not generally associated with poverty or race. Except for Indian communities and parts of southern Missouri, the out-movement generally comes from areas of high educational standards, good median incomes, and reasonable housing conditions. In effect, the rural areas of the Midwest have avoided poverty by exporting their youths.

However, the pressures on the supply of jobs within the region have not been equal. There are substantial differences in childbearing patterns that in turn produce different potential rates of labor force increase. In some areas, such as northern Missouri, southern Iowa, or southeastern Kansas, people have had comparatively small families. In such areas only a moderate rate of job growth is needed to cope with the oncoming labor force. But some other areas of different cultural and religious background have childbirth rates sufficient to double the population each generation. In these counties, the labor force would grow by more than 25 percent in the 1970s if none of the young people left. Even a partial slowdown of the out-migration rate would soon result in local population gain.

EFFECTS OF DECLINE. Data that measure the effects of decline on rural communities are not regularly reported and therefore are not easy to quantify. But several things can be said. As noted earlier, the typical process of decline is for young adults to leave the community in large proportions as they finish high school and not return. As successive classes of young people leave, the average age of the community rises and the age structure becomes rather distorted so that after awhile, the number of people in their 50s or 60s may come to exceed the number in their 20s or 30s. The birth rate begins to fall because of the shortage of young adults, and the population then ages even faster. If the median age of the population passes 35 years, deaths are likely to begin to exceed births, and a condition occurs in which the community declines in population both from migration and because there are more deaths than births.

The average age in hundreds of midwestern rural towns is now over 40 years, and in many it is over 50 years.[2] Where the latter figure applies, towns are usually small hamlets of just several hundred people, but median ages of over 40 occur in many larger places and in some entire counties. The median age of the entire U.S. population, by contrast, is 28 years. Where the median age is up into the mid-40s, the proportion of people who are 65 years old and over is a fourth or more of the total population. This is a far higher proportion of older people than is normal, and it has far-reaching effects on the context of life in such communities—for both the old and the young.

With the relative absence of families of childbearing age, the average number of people per household (or per occupied housing unit) is somewhat low. For example, the nonmetro towns of less than 1,000 population in Wisconsin, Minnesota, and South Dakota have an average household size of 2.87 persons, compared with 3.21 persons in those states as a whole. But more significant than this is the fact that average household size is declining generally, even in towns without population loss. People live longer, so we have more older, husband-wife families where the children have grown up and left. People are more financially independent in old age now and are less likely to move in with their children after retirement or widowhood than in the past. And in the younger age groups, people are less likely to remain in the parental household until marriage. The result of these factors is that small average household size requires more occupied housing units to accommodate a given population than formerly. Nationally, households are increasing at a more rapid rate than total population, so a community that is decreasing in population is not necessarily decreasing in households.

It might come as a surprise to many to learn that although the towns of less than 1,000 population in Wisconsin, Minnesota, and South Dakota had an overall decline of 0.7 percent in population during 1960–70, they had an increase of 5.3 percent in the number of occupied housing units. And whereas 62 percent of them had population declines, only 42 percent had household declines. Even among towns as small as 300–399 people, the average trends of population and household change were in opposite directions. These differences are not extreme, but they do have significance. The housing function—and the goods and services that it supports—has held up better in the small communities than total population changes would indicate.

2. In the three North Central states for which age data of small towns are published—Wisconsin, Minnesota, and South Dakota—90 places had populations with a median age of 50 years or more in 1970. Nine of these had populations with a median age of over 60 years. All the latter were places of less than 200 population.

I have not attempted to estimate information on characteristics other than age of migrants from the rural communities of the North Central region. I think it safe to say that it is widely assumed by locals and outsiders alike that many of the brightest young people leave. It is certainly true that the bulk of those leave who seek a college education or specialized occupations. Some return after college; many do not. Many of the careers open to college graduates are disproportionately located in urban areas. Throughout the Midwest, the major current educational difference between urban and rural adults of less than 50 years of age is the proportion who have gone to college, not the proportion who have completed high school. High school enrollment rates for 16- and 17-year-olds are generally higher in rural areas than in urban.

But the out-movement is not limited to the more ambitious. It has taken so large a proportion of young people, especially west of the Mississippi River, that all economic and ability classes are represented. In addition, it is clear that the educational attainment of rural populations has risen rapidly, regardless of the effects of out-migration. As an example, in Iowa the median education of the rural population in 1960 was 1.5 years less than that of the urban; by 1970 both medians had risen, but the difference had been reduced to 0.1 year by the more rapid rural rise.

Further, it cannot be said that decline of population has prevented income increases. Grouping counties in the West North Central states by population change shows that those losing population had lower average family incomes than those gaining population (Table 1.5). This accords with the typical heavy dependence on agriculture of losing counties, and shows an income rationality in the population movement. But as a class, the declining counties experienced more rapid rates of income growth from 1959–69 than did those where population was increasing. The reasons for this are not clear from the information available. The comparative returns from the 1959 and 1969 crop and livestock years could be a factor, so could the increase in employment of women in rural areas, or the shifting of the adult population in declining counties toward middle-age where income is typically at its peak. Whatever the factors, counties with decreasing population typically have an income disadvantage relative to those with increasing population in the same region. But the demographic decrease has apparently not prevented progress in attaining higher incomes and narrowing the relative income gap.

THE FUTURE. In one sense, the 1970–80 decade is the last chance that many small communities will have in the immediate future

TABLE 1.5. Median income of counties in West North Central States, 1960 and 1970, by population change, 1960–70

Population Change, 1960–70	Counties	Median Family Income		
		1970	1960	Percent change
	(number)	*($)*	*($)*	
Total[a]	619	8,985	5,154	74.3
10% gain or more	77	10,696	6,239	71.4
0–9.9% gain	127	8,835	5,237	68.7
0–9.9% loss	209	7,652	4,278	78.9
10–14.9% loss	108	6,877	3,766	82.6
15% loss or more	98	6,531	3,760	73.7

[a] Total includes St. Louis city. Values for counties with 15 percent loss or more partly estimated.

to stabilize their populations. I refer to the fact that despite the overall population loss, most small communities presently have fairly large numbers of youth 10–19 years old as a result of the high birth rates of the 1950s. In both the East and West North Central divisions, there are more rural youths of this age than there were in either 1960 or 1950 (Table 1.6).

However, the out-migration of rural adults who would now have children under 10 years old, coupled with the decline in the birth rate of the 1960s, has greatly undercut the number of very young children. In 1970, there were only 76 percent as many rural children under 5 years old in the East North Central states as there were in the 10–14 age group, and only 67 percent as many in the Plains tier of the West North Central states. The rapid decrease in the birth rate since 1970 is further reducing these proportions. Thus, once the present cohorts of rural youths now 10 years and older are out of school, the subsequent groups leaving school will be successively smaller for many years to come. If those youths reaching adulthood in the 1970s do not feel any greater attraction to remaining in the rural and small town environment than did those in the 1960s, population declines in the Midwest—especially in the western half—could become more widespread, because there will be fewer births to offset the out-migration.

In the West North Central states, the proportion of jobs that are agricultural (plus mining) continues to be high in many counties. Even after the farm consolidations of the 1960s, more than half of the West North Central counties still have more than 30 percent of their workers in farm production work. Under the pattern of economic development in recent years, such a proportion is usually too high to permit any population increase. Although I would expect somewhat faster nonextractive industry and business growth in the 1970s in these counties, it is unlikely to occur at a pace sufficient to

TABLE 1.6. Rural population under 25 years old for subdivisions of the North Central Region, 1970, 1960, and 1950

Age	East North Central Division			West North Central Division—1st tier[a]			West North Central Division—2nd tier[b]		
	1970	1960	1950	1970	1960	1950	1970	1960	1950
				(thou)					
Population by age									
Under 5 years	893.2	1,152.7	1,034.7	318.4	445.9	467.6	153.9	256.4	275.9
5–9 years	1,114.6	1,112.0	905.9	409.6	440.0	418.6	204.0	254.1	237.5
10–14 years	1,176.9	1,010.6	792.3	440.3	410.7	376.6	230.2	231.6	214.1
15–19 years	966.2	754.1	674.2	355.5	312.7	318.2	194.7	174.6	196.2
20–24 years	628.7	514.2	597.7	204.0	194.3	252.3	101.7	113.9	164.7
				(%)					
Indexes of population by age[c]									
Under 5 years	75.9	97.9	87.9	72.3	101.3	106.2	66.9	111.4	119.9
5–9 years	94.7	94.5	77.0	93.0	99.9	95.1	88.6	110.4	103.2
10–14 years	100.0	85.9	67.3	100.0	93.3	85.5	100.0	100.6	93.0
15–19 years	82.1	64.1	57.3	80.8	71.0	72.3	84.6	75.8	85.2
20–24 years	53.4	43.7	50.8	46.3	44.1	57.3	45.5	49.5	71.6

SOURCE: U.S. censuses of population.

[a] Iowa, Minnesota, Missouri.
[b] Kansas, Nebraska, North Dakota, South Dakota.
[c] Index, age group 10–14 years = 100.0

avoid further population declines in many counties or towns that are already low in population. If the statistical relationship between extractive industry employment and population change observed in the region in the 1960s were to persist in the 1970s, about 280 West North Central counties might expect to decrease in population in the 1970s. This would be less than the 415 that decreased in the 1960s. The interplay of nonextractive development trends and the birth rate will determine whether the actual number proves to be larger or smaller than this projection.

The East North Central states no longer have high exposure to population decline from lowered agricultural and mining manpower needs. Only 7 percent of the counties in this division now have even a fifth of their workers in farm or mine work. Some areas in this division will be susceptible to population decrease, but it is just as likely to be from problems with their manufacturing mix or movement out of central city counties as from agricultural or mining trends.

Many rural areas of the North Central region that have extensive districts unsuited to agriculture and well suited to recreation or retirement have been attracting population rapidly. This is especially true in the Missouri Ozarks and the lower peninsula of Michigan, and it is partly true in northern Wisconsin and Minnesota. This trend has reversed longstanding population declines in many counties and small towns. Given the increasing prevalence of steady retirement incomes among growing numbers of older people, plus the increased emphasis on recreation activity, this trend will almost certainly spread to additional areas, particularly where there are lakes—natural or otherwise—and cheap land. It is a force that is bringing many urban natives and former rural people back into rural areas, but it cannot be expected to affect all rural areas equally or materially.

The smaller the community setting examined, the more extreme its characteristics can be. For example, counties do not show as high median ages, as small average household sizes, or as extreme trends of growth or decline as some towns do. We must expect many places to continue to experience major declines, even if the larger county community of which they are a part shows increased retention of people. Data from the Fuguitt study (1963) show that size of place does not have as much association with population retention where the place is within 50 miles of a metropolitan city. The forces of population spread and redistribution that characterize most Midwestern metro cities affect villages of less than 500 people to some extent, just as they do places of several thousand. Such places may become attractive for cheap housing or as a commuting refuge from urban congestion. But away from the metro perimeters, I expect a continuation of the existing pattern of predominant population loss among very small places. Even as early as 1951, Chittick found that half of the towns in South Dakota with 250–500 population did not have drug stores, fuel dealers, or household appliance stores; two-fifths lacked banks; and a third had no eating places.[3] Such communities may be incorporated and have a sense of identity and a desire for perpetuation, but they are not generally centers with an adequate minimal range of urban services. Their origin was often the product of a limited span of years in between the railroad and automotive eras. They typically have little to attract industry. Their prospects for active survival may be dim except to serve as satellite residential and retail nodes, dependent economically on larger towns.

But by the same token, I am impressed with the ability of a majority of places of more than 500 people to retain their population. The forces that impelled metropolitan concentration of industry have been weakened, especially for manufacturing. There are many factors persuading firms to seek nonmetropolitan locations, if not for their headquarters then at least for branch plants. And the results show up clearly in employment data for the United States as a whole. The cities have lost some of their urbanity, and the rural areas have lost much rusticity. Especially among people who have finished the wandering and questing period of post-high school youth, there is an increasing willingness—if I interpret both polls and events correctly— to live in smaller-scale communities. This may be most difficult to translate into economic feasibility in the West North Central states. But the potential for demographic stability after the present inevitable period of transition to lower population levels is evident in many areas.

3. Douglas Chittick, *Growth and Decline of South Dakota Trade Centers, 1901–51*, Agricultural Experiment Station, Bulletin 448 (Brookings: South Dakota State College, 1955), p. 44.

CHAPTER TWO

THE HUMAN DIMENSION

ROBERT F. KAROLEVITZ

I AM NOT an authority in the study of rural decline, I have no revealing statistics on the subject, and I am not necessarily a tub-thumper for making little Pittsburghs out of every ex-whistlestop on the prairie.

By profession I am a free-lance writer and have been for many years. I have produced considerable publicity and promotion material for the state of Washington, the city of Seattle, the Seattle World's Fair, the Boeing Company, and numerous other political subdivisions and private enterprises. Almost always that work was geared to the luring of people, the generation of growth, and the achievement of economic gain. Progress was the slogan-word for almost every project.

Then one day—after 17 years in the Pacific Northwest—it dawned on me that my work was self-defeating when related to my own personal living goals. Every new family which one of my ads or articles might have attracted to the Puget Sound country added to the mounting people problems of pollution, traffic congestion, crime, employment, school impaction, and the decline of the salmon population.

Maybe the reaction of my wife and me was one of supreme selfishness, but when the Boeing Company moved north of Seattle to build a new plant for the production of supersonic transports and our pleasant little 5-acre retreat was threatened by engulfment, we decided abruptly that we had had it. We sold out lock, stock, and clam guns, and headed for South Dakota where we hoped never again to be caught in another people boom.

I explain this at the outset so you will at least partially under-

ROBERT F. KAROLEVITZ is a farmer, businessman, and free-lance writer, residing near Mission Hill, South Dakota.

stand what my personal philosophies and choices are. We did not *just* move to Mission Hill, South Dakota, and buy a farm. When we decided to leave Seattle with our two daughters, we made a detailed list of the characteristics we sought in a new hometown, and these included:

- Population under 20,000
- West of the Mississippi River location
- Out of the influence of a metropolitan area
- With a small college and library
- A little bit of fishing
- An adequate hospital

After completing our list, we visited such towns as Dillon, Montana; LaGrande, Oregon; Moscow, Idaho, and other qualifying locations. Then all of a sudden it came clear to us that we were really describing my old hometown of Yankton, South Dakota, and though I had insisted on numerous occasions that I would never return, I reviewed my decision and did a personal about-face.

RIGHT DECISION. We have been back in South Dakota for more than five years now and are more than ever convinced that we made the right decision. My observations, concerns, and conclusions regarding *Communities Left Behind* and the effects on the people involved will be based on what I have seen and experienced since returning to South Dakota—undoubtedly with some of my opinions colored to a degree because I am an escapee from the big city and never want to go back!

One of my first assignments following our relocation on a farm some seven miles northeast of Yankton was to write the story of Edward G. Melroe and the manufacturing company he founded in Gwinner, North Dakota. The resultant book, *E. G.—Inventor by Necessity,* tells about a small town in south central North Dakota that *should* have been a "community left behind," but it wasn't because of the imagination and leadership of Ed Melroe and his sons. They began building modified grain pickups for combines in their spare time in an old abandoned service station, just to fill local orders and to supplement the family farm income. Quoting briefly from the book:

> Gwinner itself didn't have much going for it. Counting two or three stray dogs, the salesmen who called on O. J. Dahl's grocery store and the daily bread-truck driver, the dwindling hamlet had a population of almost 200 in 1947. Less than half century old, it was the type of town which theoretical sociologists were already dooming to extinction.

. . . In its first 47 years it gave little promise of being anything more than a sleepy rail town where farmers could come to deliver their grain and do their basic shopping. . . . By every criterion, the Sargent County hamlet was a most illogical place to start a manufacturing company. It was "too far from anywhere." Everything had to be shipped in and shipped out. There simply weren't enough people to provide a labor pool. When the Melroe family decided to go into the pickup-building business in an expanded way, it was just a replay of the old story about the bumble bee which scientists said had too much weight for its wing-span and, therefore, shouldn't be able to fly—but the bumble bee didn't know this, so it flew anyhow. Totally unsophisticated in the world of industry, E. G. Melroe and sons didn't know that Gwinner was an impossible place to do business, and as a result, when they "flew anyhow," the tiny town and the entire state of North Dakota were the better for it!

Today the Melroe Company has more than twice as many employees in Gwinner than the total village population in 1947, and the firm grosses millions of dollars annually. The thriving town has a golf course, paved and lighted streets, an airport, and many other municipal improvements directly related to the company's success. I would recommend the Melroe-Gwinner story as a classic for further study about a town which should have died, but didn't.

COMMON THEME. As the result of the Melroe project, I became increasingly aware of what was and what wasn't happening in other towns and small cities in North and South Dakota, and I have seen literally a full spectrum of successes and failures. In general, the stories have a common theme. The town came into being because of river shipping, railroad expansion, land company development, and/or the marketing needs of the homesteaders in a day's wagon-trip radius around the community. A few strategically located sites became area shopping and transportation centers and thus thrived. A few others—by political maneuvering and leverage—were assigned state or other governmental institutions which provided a stable economic base. Several others found a future because of local resources: granite at Milbank, gold at Lead, lumber and various mineral deposits near Custer, productive alluvial soil for nursery stock at Yankton.

With the coming of the automobile and the decline of the railroad, many optimistically founded towns that had no special or unique economic base to sustain them began to fade. That process of decline is continuing today, in some places at an accelerated rate, and is hastened in certain areas by school reorganization and interstate highway bypassing. Wherever I have seen successful efforts to halt and reverse the trend, the one common element is invariably a somewhat unusual person (or group) with three characteristics: leadership, imagination, and gumption.

It took an idea to make the now-famous Wall Drug Store what it is today—and to keep Wall from joining the ranks of the economic failures. Because of men and women with imagination and drive in South Dakota, there is a successful gemstone manufactory in Lemmon, a candle-making industry in Isabel, agricultural equipment production in Salem, and an industrial crystal plant in Yankton. The little village of Lesterville has a thriving interstate smoked fish business. Seven of my twelve books were published not in New York, but in Aberdeen, and a special order for 107,000 copies of one of them by a Chicago advertising agency required two carloads of paper; the printing work was done in South Dakota by South Dakotans.

HUMAN INGREDIENT. I don't believe absentee ivory-tower planners can by themselves save most fading Dakota communities. In my estimation it takes the human ingredient *on the scene* to get the job done. And not every town has the leadership and the imagination required to keep it from becoming a "community left behind." Certainly, planners can provide guidelines and serve as catalysts, but a town without its own people as resources is in serious trouble from that deficiency alone.

On a slightly different tack, I admit that I am fortunate because I can do my work wherever I choose to be. Certainly my income potential is limited because I refuse to live in a big city—especially New York, Los Angeles, or Washington, D.C.—which offers a special lure to writers. But not everyone thinks as I do, and this is especially true of our younger people.

We hear a lot about out-migration of our youth these days, and in terms of human dimensions, I agree that young people are greatly affected by—and, in turn, greatly affect—the declining rural community. Another publication says:

> It is common to lament the tendency of the best men and women to leave the farm and go to the city as a modern or present-day tendency, whereas it is as old as civilization itself.
>
> Plutarch in his "Praecepta Politica" protested against the threatening invasion of large cities; Cicero thundered against the depopulation of the rural districts through similar attractions to those which draw young men and women from the farm today. Even Justinian, the great law-maker, was in favor of legislation designed to keep the people on the farm.
>
> The great Roman Emperor Augustus before the Christian era saw that his empire was being undermined and the strength of his people sapped by the exodus from the country to the city, and called to him

the poets of the nation and commanded them to sing of the beauties
and profits of country life, in order to attract his people back to the
land. This trend cityward has been to a degree due to the half education which has prevailed in the rural districts and which has given the
farm boy glimpses of the more attractive city life without teaching him
at the same time how he may obtain such a life at home.

That statement was written by H. J. Waters, president of Kansas
State Agricultural College in 1910 and was published in the *Farm and
Real Estate Journal*. More than 60 years later the condition still
exists, with additional complications, of course. The article tells of
giving "the farm boy glimpses of the more attractive city life." In
1910 the motor car was just emerging as a practical reality, and there
was no television. Today those two developments are the mixed bless-
ings of our age, and television especially has led to what I like to call
the New York–Los Angeles Syndrome, which to my mind is a social
disease.

Hundreds of copywriters—as I once was—sit in their tiny cubicles
and write commercials to beckon young people to the so-called good
life. "Come to where the action is" is a compelling theme of talk
shows, sports spectaculars, California beach movies, and even the
network news. During the World War I period someone wrote a
song entitled "How You Gonna Keep 'Em Down on the Farm After
They've Seen Paree?" That, of course, was just an inkling of what
we have experienced in recent years when, in our affluent society,
youngsters have had the wheels and the money to follow the material-
istic drummers.

To a considerable degree we reversed the frontier concept. It is
no longer popular to gamble to achieve your own little piece of freedom by the sweat of your brow. We want to bunch up; we are woe-
fully security conscious. "Enjoy the fruits of your labors *before* you
labor" is an erroneous doctrine with many disciples, and I am sure
it has an eroding effect on our rural communities, in particular.

PARADOXICAL ACTS. Meanwhile, as we decry the exodus of the
young and the decline of our smaller communities, we seem to
be making paradoxical moves as a nation. We abandon more
and more railroad trackage; we centralize our post office facilities in
larger cities in the name of efficiency; we consolidate our schools; we
build interstate freeways to whisk travelers from one population center to another; we legislate against so-called small, inefficient hospitals;
and we promote the expansion of the farm unit so fewer people are
required to produce our food and fiber. Our people move to the big
cities in pursuit of higher wages, and if that does not materialize or
the job folds, they may find it much more comfortable to apply for

unemployment, welfare, or food stamps in the anonymity of a metropolitan lineup than in one's own hometown.

Frankly, I don't have any answers except the currently unpalatable ones like hard work, self-denial, and a certain amount of discomfort. But that's the rub. Many of our big-city friends, for instance, shared our dislikes of the megalopolis, but none of them followed us in our upstream swim. And, strangely enough, many South Dakotans have told us to our faces that we were crazy to come back home. Too many people romanticize about the good old days in the towns of their youth, but they know they would never leave the city.

Reversing the trend away from rural America will be a tremendous educational job. Not only must we combat the economic realities of the day, but we must overcome a deeply ingrained materialism which seems to make people want to swarm together like bees in giant hives. Not everyone wants to go to the city, but the various economic and social demands of our so-called enlightened society keep the pressures on no matter how one tries to fend them off.

I would like to cite an example of what I have seen happening in South Dakota. When we moved onto the farm five years ago, we became involved with three other couples, all younger than us, but with all the husbands and wives at home working on their various farms and enjoying it. Today all three wives are commuters to employment in Yankton. One of the husbands is holding down a full-time job in town reading water meters, after which he rushes home to do his farming after-hours and on weekends. The other two husbands are brothers who are in partnership. While one stays home doing the work on both farms and two rental units, the other drives a petroleum transport usually more than 50 hours a week.

There are ten children—most of them now teenagers—in the three families, and the demands for teeth braces, special medical care, education, automobiles, etc., have forced a complete, unwanted change in the lives of the parents. Coupled with increased farm production costs, these pressures have brought about a situation which none of the participants favor and which has certainly had debilitating effects on the family structure. And you can be sure that very few of the ten youngsters, seeing the economic struggles of their parents, want to go through it themselves, so they are already beginning to look to more glamorous existences elsewhere.

This is all part of the human dimension of the rural problem. It's not going to be easy, and there are not going to be pat solutions. Leadership and imagination—the two most vital elements to the redirection of a declining community—cannot be pulled off an inventory shelf or spewed from a computer. Not all the "communities left behind" will survive, but I believe we will be better off if they do.

CHAPTER THREE

CONSEQUENCES OF DECLINE AND COMMUNITY ECONOMIC ADJUSTMENT TO IT

GERALD A. DOEKSEN, JOHN KUEHN, AND JOSEPH SCHMIDT

THE WELL-KNOWN publication, *The People Left Behind* [15], emphasized the problems of poverty in rural America. Since the publication of that report, a great deal of attention has been centered on the rural poor and on the fate of rural communities. President Nixon summarized conditions of rural America in a March 10, 1971, speech:

> First, in rural America itself, the loss in human resources has compounded the problems of diversifying the economy and fostering vigorous and progressive community life. Those who have chosen to stay have found it harder and harder to pay for and provide services such as good schools, health facilities, transportation systems, and other infrastructure attractive enough to keep people *in* rural America, or to lure jobs and opportunity *to* rural America. Many of the small towns which dot the countryside have to struggle for existence; they often have difficulty attracting good school teachers or physicians, many fight stagnation while most of the economy is expanding; they cannot give the older, the disadvantaged, the less educated people needed assistance and care.

Marion Clawson [8] states his feelings in another way: "It is not an exaggeration to say that rural towns are sick." With this type of prognosis for rural residents and their communities, it is not difficult to see the urgent need for action.

In this chapter we intend to: (1) delineate the economic dynamics that describe the cumulative system, (2) rationalize the reactions

GERALD DOEKSEN is an economist with the Economic Development Division, Rural Development Service, USDA, Oklahoma State University. JOE SCHMIDT is an agricultural economist, Economic Development Division, Rural Development Service, USDA, Oklahoma State University. JOHN KUEHN is an agricultural economist, Economic Development Division, Rural Development Service, USDA, University of Missouri.

of economic institutions given the historical setting, and (3) consider the future outlook for rural communities.

ECONOMIC DYNAMICS LEADING TO THE PRESENT COMMUNITY SETTING. Conventional theories of growth do not explain the present economic situation that rural communities are facing. For example, the classical theory failed to consider the exact patterning of the dynamic adjustments through time. It failed to consider the plight of old and/or poorly skilled people who did not move "correctly." However, historically based theories of regional growth can be used to explain some of the underlying causes of problems facing many rural communities. It is vital to use the historical approach in understanding rural poverty and rural community problems and the social and economic conditions which led to those undesirable conditions.

The Settlement Pattern Hypothesis. According to this hypothesis, several historical events set the stage for rural poverty and rural community problems. A version of this settlement pattern hypothesis given by Harry Caudill [5] specifies historical events that he considers instrumental in the development of the present community setting. These events are used to help explain the ensuing plight of regions such as Appalachia, the Ozarks, the Great Plains, and the South.

The first historical event influential in bringing about our current community setting was the settling of America's frontier. The frontiersmen, backwoodsmen, hunters, and adventurers were the first to venture into unsettled frontiers. After these adventurers and explorers had scouted the new territories, scratch, or temporary, farmers began to settle this new land. This group consisted largely of uneducated people and some scorned intellectuals. The frontier economy was not completely formulated until after the arrival of more permanent farmers and community builders. This group came to stay and converted the nation's raw resources into usable wealth. They developed excellent schools, built comfortable homes, and organized the communities into viable units. The social and educational differences between the temporary settlers and the permanent settlers enlarged as new frontiers were settled. Finally, all new frontiers were settled and the frontiersmen and scratch farmers had nowhere to move. According to Caudill [5] the backwoods culture is predominant in Appalachia and the Ozarks but is also present in destitute parts of other regions.

The second historical event influencing present conditions concerns initial land use and settlement. The frontier was homesteaded without regard to the productivity of the land, climate, or topography, and as a result, land was oversettled. Also, the early homesteaders were careless in their use of natural resources. They plowed up tough plains grasses, cleared land without regard to conservation, and used up natural resources rapidly. This settlement pattern is typical of what occurred in the Great Plains.

Another historic event, according to Caudill [5], was the institution of slavery. Plantation owners imported slaves as a source of labor. After emancipation, the former slaves were forced to make a living on small acreages, seek jobs as farm hands, find nonfarm jobs, or migrate to metropolitan areas. They were unprepared for their new roles. Before emancipation they had not been educated and afterwards they were often deprived of a decent education because schools were poor. The historical events surrounding slavery explain the present setting of some rural communities in the South.

Tweeten [18] proposed another settlement pattern hypothesis. His hypothesis states that the more educated, progressive, and vigorous pioneers settled in what are now the commercial farming areas. The settlers who lacked education and capital were unable to compete for the rich productive land and were forced to settle the less productive regions. These factors hindered economic growth and as a result these regions have continued to lag behind other regions. This hypothesis might be an alternative explanation to the settling of rural communities in the Ozark and Appalachian regions.

The Matrix-Location Hypothesis. Schultz, in a discussion of income disparity among regions and communities, proposed the matrix-location hypothesis [17]. His hypothesis is that economic development occurs in a specific locational matrix and that the locational matrices are largely industrial-urban at the center. He would argue that agricultural areas and communities located in close proximity to an urban center are favorably situated and are able to make the proper adjustments. The agricultural environment, located on the periphery, is situated where economic growth is not occurring satisfactorily.

Available empirical evidence does not completely support Schultz's theory. For a discussion of several studies testing some of the above hypotheses, see Tweeten [18]. Each becomes a partial theory and generally cannot be applied as the theory to explain the present setting of rural America. But each partial theory is useful for specific areas and aids in our understanding of how and why certain rural communities arrived at their present economic situation. More importantly, we are concerned with the reactions of communities to their economic situation and finally to the subject of their future.

THE INSTITUTIONAL REACTION TO THE HISTORICAL

SETTING. The historical setting becomes very important as rural residents react to their environment. Two theories are available which assist in the explanation of institutional reaction.[1] These are: (1) the rural poverty ghettoization thesis, and (2) the thesis of economic base in reverse. The rural poverty ghettoization thesis is exemplified quite clearly by the institutional reactions resulting from a decline in the Ozarks region. The economic-base-in-reverse theory is more applicable to conditions existing in the Great Plains. These theories explain how institutions react to an economic setback, and they could apply in the same way to other geographical areas as well.

Rural Poverty Ghettoization Thesis. Bender et al. [3] have recently suggested a rural poverty ghettoization thesis which explains the institutional reactions to an economic setback. The thesis proposes three interrelated subprocesses that reinforce each other in such a way that low incomes, inadequate institutions, and poverty prone people tend to accumulate to form a rural ghetto.

These subprocesses are termed as: intergenerational familial poverty, class-selective migration, and changes in the productivity of social and economic institutions. The subprocess of intergenerational poverty[2] concerns families with histories of economic and social deprivation. Succeeding generations of these families tend to remain in poverty. Class-selective migration involves the type of migrant who moves into or out of a region. The style of life in a declining region screens out certain classes of potential in-migrants and encourages out-migration of these same classes within the region. The out-migrants are the highly educated and the in-migrants are the unskilled workers with similar values, attitudes, and characteristics to those of the people left in the region. The third subprocess in the poverty ghettoization thesis is the change in the productivity of social and economic institutions. Community leaders and local officials allow private firms to "externalize" their costs, and public goods are supplied inadequately and inefficiently due to sparse population, causing the region to attract low-wage industries. Normally, these industries do not require many complementary community services and are not required to pay taxes to support the complex community infrastructure because of tax exemptions granted by the community.

1. The definition of institutions is consistent with Hildreth and Schaller's [13, p. 769], which is: "Institutions include customs, laws, and rights as well as man-made devices like materials to facilitate, guide, and control interactions between people."
2. Data were collected by Bender et al. [3] from the Ozarks region to substantiate this. For a complete presentation see [3].

Economic Base in Reverse. In many rural areas, particularly in the
Great Plains, we have very likely witnessed the reverse workings
of the economic base theory. This is specifically true when employment or population data are studied. If the economic base declines, then economic-base-in-reverse theory predicts that total employment and population will decline by some multiple. Concomitant
with this dwindling economic base, we have also observed the tendency for market areas in trades and services to become more extended
spatially.

Five major factors involved in the dynamic workings of the rural
economic system can be hypothesized. First, extraordinary changes in
agricultural technology have drastically reduced the number of people on farms—a major part of the rural economic base—while in many
instances increasing per capita income of the remaining farm population. Rural trades and services have had to enlarge their market areas
because of their dwindling population base. This holds even for the
typical small town general store, although to some extent, increasing
per capita income may have tempered the need for larger market
areas. Second, highway improvements have substantially reduced
transportation costs, including time, borne by consumers of trades
and services. This has in turn permitted the spatial growth of market
areas and the enlargement of demand zones faced by spatially competitive firms. Third, both urban and rural consumers appear to prefer
a wider range of choices when they shop. Thus the shopping center
is preferred to the general store. These newer forms of marketing
establishments probably have a threshold size considerably larger
than the more traditional small-town establishments, because of inventory costs. Fourth, the resulting changes in economies-of-size for
trades and services require greater revenues for even a minimum
threshold existence. The newer establishments must realize more
revenue by selling to more people within enlarging market areas.
Fifth, there is apparently emerging a preference for living in or near
small metropolitan areas. Thus, we have observed the flight of people
from rural to urban areas and from downtown metro areas to suburbia.

The theories have two common elements. First, class migration
is mentioned in both theories and is occurring in the Ozarks and the
Great Plains. The community educates its young people only to have
them move to areas where job opportunities exist, leaving an older,
less skilled population. Second, the communities have found it difficult to provide adequate public services because of a decreasing economic base and tax exemption policies granted new industries. This
problem is intensified because rural communities are competitive and
have not had intercommunity planning to provide adequate and efficient public services. It appears that many of the institutional reac-

tions to the historical setting have not improved the economic setting. In the attempt to determine the future of rural communities, answers to such questions as: What is the future of a particular community? Will a declining community continue to die? What can be done to assist rural communities? are vital to rural development policy makers.

Some years ago Fox [10] stated that: "The major problem of rural society in the United States is our institutionalized belief that a rural society exists and can be manipulated successfully apart from society as a whole."

The truth of this statement becomes clearer as rural communities adjust to changing conditions within the total U.S. picture. Whether a rural community will grow or decline depends upon a large number of factors. First, each community must be studied within the context of the entire nodal area to gain an understanding of its future role. Then to gain insight into each community's future, an analysis of the economic base of the region must be completed. Once the community's and the area's economic bases are established, their future can be hypothesized. Illustrations and examples will be used which are related to the Great Plains economy, but this discussion is applicable to other regions of the United States as well.

ECONOMIC BASE OF A REGION. A study of the agricultural, mineral, industrial, recreational, and human resource base of a region should indicate expected economic changes and economic potential. All of these sectors are instrumental in shaping a community's future. Several tools can assist in measuring the economic base of a region: location theory, agglomeration or diffusion, international trade theory, income convergence, interregional multipliers, economic base models, input-output models, stage or life cycle theories, central place theories, activity analysis, simulation models, and from-to analysis.[3]

An in-depth analysis of agricultural production in the Great Plains region was made by Hertsgaard [1]. Table 3.1 shows that from 1941 to 1971, the percentage of the value of U.S. crops produced in the Great Plains increased from 17.8 percent to 21.5 percent. The percentage of the value of U.S. livestock produced in the Great Plains increased from 20.7 percent to 30.3 percent. Combining crop and livestock production, the Great Plains increased its share of U.S. production from 19.0 percent to 26.2 percent.

Also during this same time period, changes occurred in the farm labor sector. The total number of farms declined from 1,164,000 in

3. For this chapter, we will not venture in depth into these models or tools. For a complete discussion of these, see [4], [9], and [14].

TABLE 3.1. Value of production, Great Plains, as a percent of U.S. total

Year	Crops	Livestock	Total
1941[a]	17.8	20.7	19.0
1964[b]	26.5	22.0	24.1
1968	25.3	24.1	24.6
1971[c]	21.5	30.3	26.2

SOURCE: [1] and [19].
[a] Average of the years 1937–46 for crops.
[b] Average of the years 1962–66 for crops.
[c] Figures for 1971 livestock represent percent of U.S. cash receipts.

1940, to 987,000 in 1950, to 715,000 in 1959, and to 605,000 in 1970. The development and adoption of new agricultural technology during agriculture's earlier days required increased services from local agribusiness firms to provide farmers with agricultural inputs. At that time, population of the small towns—whose economic function was to provide goods and services to farmers—increased even though the number of farms declined. Since then economies of size have occurred in agribusiness industries, transportation technologies have increased, and many agribusiness towns are declining in population.

In most areas of the Great Plains, the total value of minerals extracted is not significant. However, several areas do have mineral extraction activities and reserves which will be instrumental in community growth or decline.

Recreation possibilities are not creating large changes in the Great Plains nor are they expected to. Schmedemann [1] verified three hypotheses which indicate the Great Plains recreational impact. These are:

1. The bulk of the outdoor recreation occurring in the Great Plains is water-based even though the area is traditionally considered to be a semi-arid region.
2. The major portion of the economic benefits resulting from outdoor recreation accrue to the highly integrated economies of the large metropolitan areas most of which are located on the periphery or outside of the region.
3. Most of the water-based recreation developments in the Great Plains have been financed with public funds; this is logical and in most cases economically justifiable on the basis that the major portion of the benefits do not accrue to the local area in which the recreation occurs or even to the Great Plains region.

The Great Plains region traditionally accounts for a relatively small proportion of the nation's total industrial activity. While the literature abounds with examples of the impact of manufacturing products on the early development of the Great Plains [23], manufacturing activity was generally external to the region. Manufacturing employment in the Great Plains grew from 367,00 in 1929 to 1,252,000 in 1971. As a percentage of total U.S. manufacturing employment this was 3.6 percent in 1929 and 6.7 percent in 1971. For a complete discussion of growth in manufacturing activity in the Great Plains see [1, 11, and 20.]

Industrial location in rural and partially rural counties is gaining momentum. Claude C. Haren [12] makes this clear when he states that:

> Rural and partly rural counties gained manufacturing jobs at a rate of 4.6 percent annually between 1959 and 1969, or more than double the ratio in the metro units. Nearly 900,000 manufacturing workers were added, together with almost another 500,000 in the remaining non-metro counties. This brought the non-metro share of total U.S. manufacturing employment up from 21 percent in 1959 to 23 percent 10 years later.

Another study [6], which analyzed industry location in Oklahoma from 1963 to 1971, supports the contention that decentralization is occurring in the manufacturing sector. In Oklahoma, from 1963 to 1971, 66.1 percent of all manufacturing jobs created by new manufacturing plants were in communities of less than 10,000 population. This trend could have a significant future impact on the communities of the Great Plains states.

THE COMMUNITY ANALYSIS. The future of each community depends largely on the economic base of its area combined with the vagaries of remote facets of national social and economic life. Once these conditions are known, communities can be classified. Barkely [2] classifies communities into four types: growth and development, growth and attenuation, decline and attenuation, and decline and development. However, classification of communities according to their hypothesized *roles* can facilitate planning and enable the communities to plan for adjustments.[4] We will use the following community classifications: recreational, resource extraction, satellite, viable trade centers, and miscellaneous.

Recreational Communities. Although there are not a great many recreational areas in the Great Plains, a few places may develop as recreational communities. Generally, these will arise around lake areas within driving distances of major metropolitan areas. The likelihood of total recreational complexes for families

4. A recent study completed by Dean F. Schreiner [16] illustrates how an analysis of the economic base can be useful in planning solid waste services.

and/or the development of second homes in the Great Plains is questionable, and in the absence of such developments secondary impacts on local economies will probably be minor.

Recreational communities can expect growing pains in the future as urban people with more money and leisure continue to seek open space and outdoor activities. Community leaders should be concerned with providing an environment that will attract weekend recreationists and urban people desiring a second home. Also, the community can usually expect a cyclical economy, which makes planning difficult. Proper zoning and the provision of adequate public services are extremely important. Planning public services in a cyclical economy is difficult because during the peak season many public services will be operating at full capacity and during the off season will be underutilized.

Resource Extraction Communities. These communities include mining, lumbering, or fishing towns and are sometimes referred to as company towns. Their function is to provide services to the company extracting the resource. These communities can be experiencing either growth or decline. The number of communities of this type in the Great Plains is small and suggestions for these communities are quite similar to those for the next two community types.

Satellite Communities. Rural America offers advantages not available in most metro areas, consequently many satellite communities have developed. Broadly defined, a satellite community is one in which a substantial proportion of the labor force works in a larger nearby town. One reason satellite communities are becoming popular is that land values are lower in rural areas. Other reasons are that many families are searching for open space and trying to get away from the stress of urban living, and technological changes have occurred in the transportation and communication sectors enabling families living in rural communities to commute to work in metropolitan centers. Satellite communities might spring up within 30 to 50 miles of urban centers. The number of metropolitan centers of 50,000 or more in the Great Plains is small (Figure 3.1); thus the expected number of satellite communities in this region is also small.

To illustrate how satellite communities have grown in recent years, population data were collected for 68 satellite communities in Oklahoma. Included in this sample were all incorporated communities and all unincorporated communities of 1,000 or more population within 30 miles of Oklahoma City and Tulsa as reported in the 1970 population census. For exact data see [20]. The population data for these communities are summarized in Table 3.2. During 1940–50, the population of these 68 communities decreased 0.8 percent, whereas

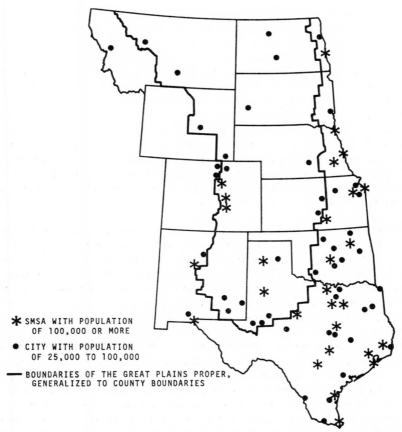

FIG. 3.1.   Larger cities and metropolitan centers in the Great Plains states.

On the map (legend):

✳ SMSA WITH POPULATION
  OF 100,000 OR MORE

● CITY WITH POPULATION
  OF 25,000 TO 100,000

— BOUNDARIES OF THE GREAT PLAINS PROPER,
  GENERALIZED TO COUNTY BOUNDARIES

TABLE 3.2.   Growth or decline of satellite communities located within 30 miles of Oklahoma City and Tulsa, 1941–50, 1951–60, 1961–70

	1941–50	1951–60	1961–70
Number of satellite communities that lost population	33	35	11
Number of satellite communities that gained population	35	33	57
Total number of satellite communities	68	68	68
Percent change in aggregate population for satellite communities	−0.8	+41.3	+42.5

SOURCE: [20].

during the 1950–60 and 1960–70 decades the population of these communities increased 41.3 percent and 42.5 percent respectively.

Satellite communities will face growth problems as families continue to seek open space. Leaders in these communities need to plan for a growing population while their main concern will be to provide an attractive environment for their residents. The satellite community probably will not become a large trade center; thus emphasis should be on making the community a nice place in which to live. Two actions are necessary for continued growth and to make the community more attractive for urban families seeking open space. These are: (1) proper zoning to aid in the creation of an attractive community, and (2) provision of quality public services at a low cost. In some cases, satellite communities should cooperate with other neighboring communities to provide adequate low-cost public services.

Viable Trade Centers. Viable trade centers make up a very small portion of the rural communities in the Great Plains. This situation also applies to other predominantly agricultural regions such as the Midwest. In all cases, the economic base of the area is largely agriculturally oriented. The settlement pattern discussed earlier indicates that the region was oversettled, and that communities arose early in the nineteenth century to provide agribusiness services to farmers and ranchers. Since then, the number of farms has greatly declined.

Like farms, agribusiness firms have experienced economies of size. For example, an implement dealer in a small community finds it expensive to have a full line of spare parts for all farm machinery because his volume is small and many parts remain in inventory a long time. Large fertilizer dealers can purchase fertilizer in carload lots, but a dealer in a small community does not have the sales volume to order in this quantity. Also, the farmer's wife now travels to larger urban centers to obtain the same variety and quality of goods as the urban wife.

The combination of these factors has meant that many rural communities have suffered a large reduction in volume of business. The alternatives facing the smaller communities will be discussed in the next section. Here we are concerned with the trade center which will survive and serve the agricultural areas. The population of these trade centers will probably range from about 5,000 to over 50,000 depending upon the trade areas involved. Distances between viable trade centers could be up to 60 miles, depending upon the density of the population. A viable trade center would be large enough to provide agribusiness inputs to farmers and ranchers at competitive prices.

The viable trade centers, as they emerge, will probably experience population growth. These trade centers are large enough or will grow to a sufficient size to have resources or markets economically attractive to manufacturing firms that may desire to decentralize. Leaders of viable trade centers should first attempt to provide quality public services at least cost. Also, they should attempt to attract industry which will have an economic linkage with the area, thus increasing secondary impacts.

The Remaining Communities. The remaining smaller communities— those of less than 2,500 population which do not fit into the above classification scheme—will have the most difficulty making adjustments. These were the communities which sprang up along with viable trade centers to serve agriculture during the settlement days. With a smaller number of farmers to serve and improved transportation, the small community lost much of its trade area to the viable trade centers. Once the decline began, it was very difficult to turn around or even stop.

The businesses of a small community are highly interdependent. The cafe depends upon the co-op elevator and the bank depends upon both. If the elevator closes up shop, the economic positions of the remaining businesses are much weaker. Also, the salvage value of dwellings, business establishments, and social service capital is very low in a declining community [7]. For example, when two elevators of neighboring communities combine, the salvage value of the unused one is very low. Also, the personal adjustment problems of residents of small towns are likely to be difficult if they are forced to seek other occupations.

It appears that a large number of these communities have made the biggest part of the adjustment. Data were collected for 431 communities in Oklahoma which are not satellite to Tulsa or Oklahoma City. They were incorporated communities with populations of under 2,500 and unincorporated communities with populations between 1,000 and 2,500. Several of the 341 communities may qualify as recreational communities, resource extraction communities, or satellite communities to viable trade centers. We feel the population data in Table 3.3 yield a fair indication of what is occurring in the smaller communities. Of the 341 communities, 239 lost population during 1940–50, 245 lost population during 1950–60, and 132 lost population during 1960–70. The data on the number of smaller communities appear to indicate that the majority of them lost population during the 1940s and 50s and gained population during the 1960s. The percentage change in aggregate population for these 341 communities supports this statement. During 1941–50, the population of these communities decreased 3.3 percent and 4.8 percent during 1951–60 but increased 7.9 percent during 1961–70. Comparing the data on satellite communities (Table 3.2) with the data on small nonsatellite com-

TABLE 3.3. Growth or decline of smaller communities in Oklahoma, 1941–50, 1951–60, 1961–70[a]

	1941–50	1951–60	1961–70
Number of small communities that lost population	239	245	132
Number of small communities that gained population	102	96	209
Total number of small communities	341	341	341
Percent change in aggregate population for small communities	−3.3	−4.8	+7.9

[a] Includes incorporated places of under 2,500 population and unincorporated places between 1,000 and 2,500 population that are not within 30 miles of Oklahoma City or Tulsa.

munities (Table 3.3), the satellite communities began their growth in the 1950s and it carried on into the 1960s, whereas the small nonsatellite communities began to grow in the 1960s. Also, the magnitude of growth is much greater for the satellite communities than for the small nonsatellite communities.

Given that the population of many of the smaller communities has leveled off and some are still declining slightly, what can be done to assist them in adjusting to this setting? One constructive approach is to encourage the leaders of these smaller communities to cooperate in planning and providing community services. Community leaders must visualize their community's role in the total area; they cannot expect their communities to perform the functions of the viable trade centers or larger metropolitan areas. The community function will most likely focus upon school districts, postal services, and quick-stop food stores. If the communities are relatively close to a viable trade center, their chances of stability or even growth may be quite high. In this case, the community leaders should attempt to use intercommunity planning to make their small community an attractive place to live. An example would be to encourage a county-wide solid waste system. This would often be much cheaper than an individual system for each community.

Leaders of a small community some distance from a viable growth center should realize that their community's potential for growth is very low and that they will not be able to keep their young people in the community. The leaders probably will desire to provide the best public services possible with the available resources. Again, intercommunity planning is a must as economies of size exist in many public services. The leaders and residents of small communities should realize that their communities may not be able to grow and that many will continue their current trends.

REFERENCES

1. Badger, Daniel D., ed. 1970. Attaining economic development, how the Great Plains can contribute to the U.S. economy. Great Plains Agricultural Council Publication No. 49.
2. Barkely, Paul W. 1972. The economic analysis of small areas: Intellectual poverty within intellectual plenty. Proceedings of a joint meeting of the Western Agricultural Economics Research Council's Committee on Community and Human Resource Development and the Western Social Research Advisory Committee, October 1971, San Francisco, Oregon State University.
3. Bender, Lloyd D., Green, Bernal L., and Campbell, Rex R. 1971. The process of rural poverty ghettoization. Paper presented to the American Association for Advancement of Science, 28 December 1971, Philadelphia, Pennsylvania.
4. Berry, Broun J. L. 1967. Strategies, models and economic theories of development in rural regions. Agricultural Economics Report No. 127, E.R.S., U.S.D.A.
5. Caudill, Harry. 1965. Reflections on poverty in America. In Arthur E. Shostak and William Gomberg, eds., *New Perspectives on poverty*. Englewood Cliffs, N.J.: Prentice-Hall.
6. Childs, Dan M. 1973. An economic analysis of plant location by community size in Oklahoma. Unpublished M.S. thesis, Oklahoma State University.
7. Clawson, Marion. 1968. *Policy directions for U.S. agriculture, long range choices in farming and rural living*. Resources for the Future, Inc. Baltimore: Johns Hopkins Univ. Press.
8. ———. 1968. *Suburbia land conversion in the U.S.* Resources for the Future, Inc. Baltimore: Johns Hopkins Univ. Press.
9. Doeksen, Gerald A., and Schreiner, Dean F. 1973. Interindustry models for rural development research. Oklahoma State Experiment Station Bulletin in process.
10. Fox, Karl A. 1962. The major problem of rural society. In *Our rural problems in their national setting*. Report containing paper presented at the Third Annual Farm Policy Review Conference, December 1962 at Ames, Iowa.
11. Fuchs, Victor R. 1962. *Changes in the location of manufacturing in the United States since 1923*. New Haven: Yale Univ. Press.
12. Haren, Claude C. 1974. Location of industrial production and distribution. In *Rural industrialization: Problems and potentials*. North Central Regional Center for Rural Development. Ames: Iowa State Univ. Press.
13. Hildreth, R. J., and Schaller, W. Neill. 1972. Community development in the 1970's. *Am. J. Agr. Econ.* 54:764–72.
14. Isard, Walter I. 1960. *Methods of regional analysis*. Cambridge: Massachusetts Institute of Technology Press.
15. President's National Advisory Commission on Rural Poverty. 1967. *The people left behind*. Washington, D.C.: U.S. Government Printing Office.
16. Schreiner, Dean F., and Muncrief, George. 1972. Estimating regional information systems. With application to Community Service Planning. *Reg. Sci. Perspectives* 2:136–58.

17. Schultz, T. W. 1953. *The economic organization of agriculture.* New York: McGraw-Hill.
18. Tweeten, Luther G. 1968. Rural poverty, incidence causes and cures. Oklahoma State Agricultural Experiment Station Processed Series P-590.
19. U.S. Department of Agriculture. 1972. *Agricultural statistics, 1972.* Washington, D.C.: U.S. Government Printing Office.
20. U.S. Department of Commerce, Bureau of the Census, 1960 and 1970. *Number of inhabitants, Oklahoma.* Washington, D.C.: U.S. Government Printing Office.
21. U.S. Department of Labor, Bureau of Labor Statistics. *Employment and earnings, states and areas.* Various issues.
22. Voelher, Stanley W. 1971. Population change and net migration by counties in the Great Plains states, 1960–70. North Dakota Agricultural Economics Report No. 73.
23. Webb, Walter Prescott. 1931. *The Great Plains.* New York: Grosset and Dunlap.

CHAPTER FOUR

CONSEQUENCES OF DECLINE AND SOCIAL ADJUSTMENT TO IT

KENNETH P. WILKINSON

HAVE YOU HEARD this one [22]:

> The country town of the great American farming region is the perfect flower of self-help and cupidity standardized on the American plan. Its name may be Spoon River or Gopher Prairie, or it may be Emporia or Centralia or Columbia. The pattern is substantially the same, and is repeated several thousand times and with a faithful perfection which argues that there is no help for it, that it is worked out by uniform circumstances over which there is no control, and that it wholly falls in with the spirit of things and answers to the enduring aspirations of the community. The country town is one of the great American institutions, perhaps the greatest, in the sense that it has had and continues to have a greater part than any other in shaping public sentiment and giving character to American culture.
>
> . . . the country-town system of prescriptive holdovers has gone into action as the safe and sane body of American common sense; until it is now self-evident to American public sentiment that any derangement of these holdovers would bring the affairs of the human race to a disastrous collapse. And all the while the material conditions are progressively drawing together into such shape that this plain country-town common sense will no longer work.

Or what about this one [18]:

> The family that wants to remain in Vandalia, far from being insulated from the tensions and threats of the outer world, is resisting economic, social, and technological forces that could break the community apart and send the pieces flying in all directions.

KENNETH P. WILKINSON is Associate Professor of Rural Sociology, Pennsylvania State University.

43

I'll try one more [1]:

> A few years ago we had a development corporation, but only five of us joined and we didn't do anything. We didn't really want new business because they would just take away consumers [sic] from us. We couldn't seem to get any money together to interest new industries. One problem is that the bankers and the retired folk control most of the money. Mr. Clayton (the banker) won't invest because he's not convinced this town can ever recuperate and the retired folk won't invest in this town 'cause their children have all left. They would rather sit on their money 'til they die so their kids—whoever they are—can inherit it.

Community decline, like community development, is a pervasive process reflected at all levels in a local society—in the demographic and ecological responses through which a population seeks to balance its size with its sustenance organization [10, 21], in the institutional patterns and organizational structures through which daily social life is lived, in the efforts of groups to alter or improve local conditions of life, and in the feelings people have about the local society [25]. This chapter focuses upon the institutional-organizational level. At that level my purpose is to describe the social processes which accompany loss of population, decreased collective viability, and lessening of the collective spirit or sense of community.

STRUCTURAL DIFFERENTIATION. At this institutional-organizational level, the critical process in the positive, developmental sense is called structural differentiation; the opposite of which must be termed de-differentiation, or simply decreased differentiation. By whatever term, the latter is a relative concept. It is generally well established (see [27]) that the basic direction of change in human social organization is toward increased differentiation. Therefore, decreased differentiation only has meaning within the context of analysis of a limited geographic area. The larger area, of which the local one is a part, is assumed to be undergoing a process of increased differentiation at the same time the local area is undergoing decreased differentiation. It may be assumed that the geographic base of the community's social structure is expanding [15]. Functions and services formerly provided in the small town or village are now being provided on a more differentiated and specialized basis in an expanded setting. What "declines" in this circumstance is the level of services available in the immediate area.

I will give three examples of what I mean. First, consider the agricultural trade center of 100 years ago in this country [6]. A place of perhaps 1,000 population or less provided all of the services and interaction opportunities outside the family people in the area were likely to require or expect. For practical purposes, the entire table of organization [3] of the society was more or less reflected in the village social structure. With increased differentiation in the larger society and increased effectiveness of transportation and communications facilities, people became aware of improved and seemingly more adequate goods and opportunities in the next town and city. As they began to go to the next town with increasing frequency to trade and interact, the agricultural village became more or less obsolete as the life of the community of which it was part became much more complex.

As a second example, consider Bellefonte, Pennsylvania, a county seat town with 7,000 population studied recently by Pierce Lewis [17]. It was established in 1790 as a trade center for the rich Nittany Valley, an agricultural area at the edge of the Allegheny plateau. The town played a role of national prominence through much of the nineteenth century in the production of pig iron which was much in demand during the Civil War, and as the hometown of several national leaders. At its peak in the 1860s, Bellefonte was a center of high culture and the site of construction of some of the most elegant, stately buildings in the East. By the end of the nineteenth century, iron prices had fallen sharply, out-migration had begun, and the finely constructed buildings changed hands and fell into disrepair. By the 1930s, demolition of many old buildings was underway. Following World War II, the GI Bill and a new ordnance research installation began to transform a neighboring village, State College, from a muddy, isolated outpost into a major growth center. The State College area—State College, University Park, and surrounding suburbs—now has a population of about 60,000. The county population is 100,000. Bellefonte continues as county seat, but one by one its services and functions have been taken over by State College. Many Bellefonte residents now travel to State College to work. Most county offices have moved their headquarters to State College. Four years ago State College got its own liquor stores. A new, modern branch of the county hospital opened in State College leaving the older, less adequate facility, which had served the county previously, in downtown Bellefonte. In brief, Bellefonte is rapidly becoming a working class suburb of State College. In the early 1950s according to Lewis [17], this trend was deeply resented by Bellefonte residents; but during the past 20 years, they have become resigned to it and have even begun to emulate the life of their upstart neighbor. Architectural masterpieces are being torn down to make way for "quick-food joints," parking lots, and service stations such as characterize State College's "main drag."

A third example of the transfer of functions to a larger area is taken from a study of six villages in Wisconsin by Bert Adams [1]. He was able to document the process of loss of functions as occurring in the following steps:

> First to leave are the specialized professionals, especially dentists, then doctors and lawyers. They move to larger places or centralized clinics on the correct assumption that a regional clientele will seek them out. Second, large dry goods establishments close down, leaving the sale of new cars to garages, with the cars on order rather than in stock, and the sale of appliances to the general dry goods store or hardware store. People will travel several miles to buy items such as cars, refrigerators, and couches, and the regional competition drives out the small town outlet early. Simultaneously, specialized services such as beauty parlors, laundries, paint stores, and television repair shops fold. Third, duplicate businesses are driven out by competition for a contracting clientele. If there are two hardware stores one may go under; if there are three groceries one or two may close. The same is true for filling stations, feed stores, and other retail establishments.

In each of these examples, there was an increase in the level of differentiation of social organization in the regional community or the larger society, but there was a decrease in the level of differentiation of social organization—particularly as regards public services— in the restricted, original community area. On the surface it might appear that what is being described is merely a natural ecological adjustment out of which will emerge a more adaptive mode of economic and social organization using improved technology. It may seem that over the long run the aggregate social welfare will be served by these changes. Simon and Gagnon [20] state it thusly:

> The land and economy of the United States will not support as many small towns as they did before. It is very difficult not to see the future as a long drawn-out struggle for community survival, lasting for half a century, in which some battles may be won but the war will be lost. A future in which most such towns will become isolated or decayed, in which the local amenities must deteriorate, and in which there will finally be left only the aged, the inept, the very young—and the local power elite.

The argument goes that the passing of the small town and the rise of the regional growth center, consistent with the principle of agglomeration [9], should be heralded as evidence of the continued progress and unilinear evolution of civilization.

But this interpretation is questioned by two facts. The first is that this is not a universal process among small communities, but one which can apparently be arrested under certain conditions with no loss in the rate of increase in social differentiation or in aggregate social welfare. The second is that there are severe social and psychological consequences of the transition in communities experiencing loss of functions and structures to larger centers, and if counted as "costs," these consequences might outweigh the calculated "benefits" of the transition.

Considering the first fact, Fuguitt [7] has noted a pronounced flattening in 1960–70 of the regression of size on growth in incorporated nonmetropolitan places. What is apparently happening is that the growth rates are slowing down in the larger places and picking up somewhat in many of the smaller ones. Certainly the smaller places are not disappearing. In the comparison of the Northeast with the rest of the United States, there appears to be evidence that once a high level of urbanization-centralization-agglomeration is reached, the positive association between community growth rate and community size (found persistently in such urbanizing areas as the Midwest, for example) tends to be muted and the regression curve flattened and even reversed. In much of Pennsylvania [8] for example, smaller places are growing more rapidly than larger places. Decentralization is apparently occurring even around nonmetropolitan centers [7]. We have known for some time that many more people would prefer to live in smaller places than actually live in them [4], and some of us have assumed that inadequate provision of services, amenities, and economic opportunities in smaller places has prevented the majority from acting upon their stated preferences. What the recent growth-size data may be showing us is that in highly urbanized areas where rural development in the sense of jobs, services, and associational structures has taken place, people are beginning to act upon those preferences. Speculative though such a theory might be, it posits a relationship which bears watching in the rest of the country.

LOCAL LEADERSHIP. Further, there have been cases in which collective efforts of local leaders were successful in retarding the process of population decline, and others in which higher levels of living and more adequate levels of public services were acquired by community residents during periods of stable or even declining population size. Charles Walker [24] has described concerted efforts by local leaders to prevent the seemingly inevitable loss of a community's steel mills. Those efforts failed, but sufficient organized effort had been generated to influence new industries to locate in the town and others to expand their operations. Studies of Tupelo, Mississippi [14], have described in detail the process by which highly committed local leaders and an effective development organization have succeeded in overcoming shortcomings in location, natural resources, and population base to carry out a comprehensive program of community development. Simon and Gagnon's [20] conclusion about the future of small towns in the United States ignores their own finding that of three villages studied, in Spiresburg, the one with the fewest resources, the efforts of leaders to secure new industrial plants resulted in four new locations during the period studied. At least three of the small places studied by Adams [1] appear to have been experiencing development, albeit with substantial assists coming from outside the community. It would seem reasonable to conclude that even if there is an underlying tendency toward regional agglomeration of community functions and structures, there is enough free variance in the relationship to leave room for intervention through purposive social action.

"COSTS" OF DECLINE. Social and psychological "costs" of community decline are manifested in many and often subtle ways.

One such cost is related to the distinction that is sometimes made between measures of the "point of emanation" of a service and the "point of utilization" of a service.[1] This is to say that the volume of services and organizations in an area differs from the level of involvement of the people of the area in those services or organizations. Quality of life indicators presumably should deal primarily with the latter [16]. Centre County, Pennsylvania, which contains Bellefonte and State College, now has a modern hospital with many specialities and superb emergency facilities; but for many people in Bellefonte, actual health care and easy access to the county service have declined. The social costs of space and access need to be carefully tabulated. I am referring here to the effects of having to travel to receive a service upon the social and personal condition of the recipient of that service.

Another social cost about which we know very little is the effect expansion of the geographic base of institutional and formal organizational functioning has upon informal aspects of social organization. Informal aspects include such things as neighboring, mutual identity, and voluntary collective action potentials. Most theories of community relate such phenomena to the facts of face-to-face experience in daily life within a relatively small locality [11]. It is important to ask whether a sense of community can emerge from the formal exchange relations which appear to be developing in the regionally organized local society. The lack of a sense of community is noted daily in news reports on various aspects of the relationship between Bellefonte and State College, and this would appear to be a substantial social cost.

Most consequences of the transfer of functions outside the local residence area are social-psychological in character and are manifested

1. This distinction, first suggested by Garrey E. Carruthers, agricultural economist of New Mexico State University, is being used in the construction of quality of life indicators on Western Regional Experiment Station Project, W-114, "Institutional Structures for Improving Rural Community Services."

in the attitudes and value expressions of local leaders and others. One feeling frequently expressed is frustration, often coupled with resentment. Cottrell [5], in his study, "Death by Dieselization," describes the reactions of residents of a community in the Southwest that was formed to service and man steam locomotives. The community was faced finally with loss of employment of up to one-third of its labor force as the railroad company switched to diesel engines which require servicing at less frequent intervals. The life of the community had been organized around the distinctive rhythms of railroad life. The local culture incorporated the myths as well as the facts of railroad operation. As Cottrell [5] observed:

> When make-work rules contributed [sic] to the livelihood of the community, the support of the churches, and the taxes which maintain the schools; when featherbed practices determine the standard of living, the profits of the businessman and the circulation of the press; when they contribute to the salary of the teacher and the preacher; they can no longer be treated as accidental, immoral, deviant or temporary. Rather they are elevated into the position of emergent morality and law.

Although the technological base on which the community depended was extremely vulnerable to changes in the larger society, this did not prevent people from organizing their lives in accordance with that base. The local social system which people had been taught to revere was suddenly no longer relevant. According to Cottrell [5]:

> . . . Those in Caliente whose behavior most nearly approached the ideal taught are hardest hit by the change. On the other hand, those seemingly farthest removed in conduct from that ideal are either rewarded or pay less the costs of change than do those who follow the ideal more closely.

Where, in such a situation, asks Cottrell, is justice?

As a result of the implicit frustration of living in a town which is somehow out of phase with trends and forces in the larger society, community residents have been observed by some researchers to develop an attitude of ambivalence toward the outside. In Springdale, for example, Vidich and Bensman [23] recorded a negative image of urban life coupled "with respect for the power, the wealth and the legitimacy of urban values." Residents were said to use a "technique of particularization" by which specific outside dependencies were recognized while the general state of extra-local dependency of the community was ignored or denied. However, in his study of small villages, Adams [1] found a tendency for the individual "to *project* or generalize his own experience—whether success or failure—rather than particularizing it."

Dissonance was reduced in either case; frustration and anxiety were handled by selectively distorting one's image of the community's extra-local relationships. Adams [1] identified accuracy of one's perception of this relationship as one of two key social psychological factors influencing the successful adaptation of the declining community resident. The local businessman who keeps up with national economic news and anticipates changes in regional supply and demand has a much better chance of successful adaptation than does one who ignores all but local conditions. If several local businessmen maintain an extra-local orientation, the local economy may be stabilized even though the population may continue to decline. A second dimension of the decline psychology described by Adams [1] is a lack of willingness to take risks. This is seen directly in reluctance to invest money in industrial parks or to take any action which might encourage the infusion of new ideas, resources, or people into the community. Simon and Gagnon [20] referred to this as a lack of commitment of leaders to the future of their towns.

One of the fundamental insights of modern social psychology is that attitudes may serve functionally for individuals. For example, a certain attitude may help an individual cope with an objectively threatening reality [13]. Case study literature provides us with a picture of community decline characterized by frustration, anxiety, ambivalence, cognitive distortion, negativism, and conservatism. Surely these must be regarded as costs rather than benefits of the expanded geographic base of institutional and organizational functioning that we have been striving for.

HUMAN WELFARE. It would appear that the time has come for us to divert our collective energies from the search for strategies to maximize structural differentiation and economic development to the search for strategies to identify and maintain the minimum levels of structural differentiation and economic development necessary to support the kinds of human community activity we want. Differentiation is a limited goal in the higher quest for human welfare, and growth and proliferation of services, infrastructure, voluntary associations, extra-local linkages, and economic opportunities may be required to move residents of some communities in America up to the basic sustenance threshold. However, continued growth and proliferation of these beyond the sustenance threshold will result in reduced rather than increased likelihood of social well-being.

The rational economic and agglomeration forces stimulating the processes of community decline are geared to providing what I would terms the means or sustenance requirements for freeing man from his lower-order or deficit needs so he can direct his attention and energies to his human potentials [2, 19]. Beyond the threshold at which these needs are adequately met, I would argue that further attention to the production of means would lessen opportunities for achieving the end of human actualization. This end would consist of conditions including distributive justice, openness of communication, tolerance, interpersonal communion, collective viability, and, at the core, respect and authentic comportment toward self and others. None of these are encouraged beyond the minimum threshold through application of economies of scale; they are encouraged through the creation of institutions and community settings of human scale. Economic growth becomes obsessive hoarding, and proliferation of services and amenities goes far beyond need in the quest for luxuries and symbols of superiority. Such would interfere with the actualization of human potentials as surely as would a sustenance deficit [26].

We should be able to deploy our existing technology and intelligence to help us escape the trap we apparently have gotten into with the agglomeration principle; and indeed there are attempts underway to do so at least on a limited scale [12]. What is needed, however, is a widely applicable procedure for enabling people to live in small communities without sacrificing the really fundamental benefits of the economies of scale concept. Many of the alleged benefits are no doubt superfluous; others seem to constitute essential conditions for human welfare.

What I have said is that (1) community decline at the institutional-organizational level means a transfer of functions from the local to the regional or larger area in response to general societal trends toward structural differentiation and attendant processes of specialization and increased efficiency; (2) such a transfer, while adaptive from the standpoint of agglomeration and economies of scale, does not provide a universal guarantee of enhanced human well-being but rather operates differently from community to community with sufficient free variance to allow for purposive intervention and tends to have social and social-psychological consequences which, from some perspectives, outweigh the presumed benefits; and (3) that we should apply our scientific efforts to the search for ways to maximize human well-being.

REFERENCES

1. Adams, Bert N. 1969. The small trade center: Processes and perceptions of growth or decline. In Robert Mills French, ed. *The community: A comparative perspective*. Itasca, Ill.: F. E. Peacock Publishers.
2. Allport, Gordon. 1955. *Becoming*. New Haven: Yale Univ. Press.
3. Arensberg, Conrad M. 1961. The community as object and as sample. *Am. Anthropol.* 63:241–64.

4. Commission on Population Growth and the American Future. 1972. *Population and the American future.* New York: Signet.
5. Cottrell, W. F. 1951. Death by dieselization: A case study in the reaction to technological change. *Am. Soc. Rev.* 16:358–65.
6. Eberts, Paul R. 1971. A theoretical perspective toward an action-oriented model of community change and development. Unpublished paper presented to the joint meetings of the Western Agricultural Economics Research Council and the Western Social Research Advisory Council, San Francisco, 13–14 October 1971.
7. Fuguitt, Glenn V. 1971. The places left behind: Population trends and policy for rural America. *Rural Soc.* 36:449–70.
8. Gingrich, Neil B. 1972. Population of Pennsylvania by county and minor civil subdivisions. University Park, Pa.: Report 100, Department of Agricultural Economics and Rural Sociology.
9. Hansen, Niles M. 1970. *Rural poverty and the urban crisis: A strategy for regional development.* Bloomington: Indiana Univ. Press.
10. Hawley, Amos H. 1950. *Human ecology: A theory of community structure.* New York: Ronald Press.
11. Hillery, George, Jr. 1968. *Communal organizations.* Chicago: Univ. of Chicago Press.
12. Kanter, Rosabeth Moss. 1972. *Commitment and community: Communities and utopias in sociological perspective.* Cambridge, Mass.: Harvard Univ. Press.
13. Katz, Daniel. 1960. The functional approach to the study of attitudes. *Public Opin. Quart.* 24:163–204.
14. Kaufman, Harold F. 1970. Team leadership: A key to development: Another chapter in the Tupelo story. State College, Miss.: Applied Series 1, Social Science Research Center, Mississippi State University.
15. Kaufman, Harold F., and Wilkinson, Kenneth P. 1967. Community structure and leadership: An interactional perspective in the study of community. State College, Miss.: Bulletin 13, Social Science Research Center, Mississippi State University.
16. Land, Kenneth C. 1971. On the definition of social indicators. *Am. Soc.* 6:322–25.
17. Lewis, Pierce, F. 1972. Small town in Pennsylvania. In John Fraser Hart, ed. *Regions of the United States.* New York: Harper and Row.
18. Lyford, Joseph P. 1962. *The talk in Vandalia: The Life of an American town.* New York: Harper Colophon Books.
19. Maslow, A. H. 1954. *Motivation and personality.* New York: Harper and Brothers.
20. Simon, William, and Gagnon, John H. 1967. The decline and fall of the small town. *Trans-action* 4:51.
21. Sly, David F. 1972. Migration and the ecological complex. *Am. Soc. Rev.* 37:615–28.
22. Veblen, Thorstein. 1969. The case of America: The country town. In David W. Minar and Scott Greer, eds. *The concept of community: Readings with interpretations.* Chicago: Aldine Publishing Co.
23. Vidich, Arthur J., and Bensman, Joseph. 1958. *Small town in mass society: Class, power, and religion in a rural community.* Garden City, N.Y.: Doubleday and Co.
24. Walker, Charles. 1955. *Steeltown.* New York: Harper and Brothers. (Cited in James S. Coleman. 1971. Community disorganization and conflict. In Robert K. Merton and Robert Nisbet, eds. *Contemporary social problems,* 3rd ed. New York: Harcourt Brace Jovanovich.)

25. Wilkinson, Kenneth P. 1970. The community as a social field. *Soc. Forces* 48:311–22.
26. ———. 1973. The concept of social well-being: Alternative frameworks for evaluating purposive action programs concerned with water resources. A paper prepared for a conference on The Social Well-Being—Quality of Life Dimension in Water Resources Planning and Development, Logan, Utah, 10–12 July 1973.
27. Young, Frank W., and Young, Ruth C. 1960. Social integration and change in twenty-four Mexican villages. *Econ. Dev. and Cultural Change* 8:366–70.

CHAPTER FIVE

FAMILY ADJUSTMENT UNDER COMMUNITY DECLINE

MARGARET J. BUBOLZ

THE TITLE of this chapter contains the assumption that the family is affected by what happens in the community and larger society; it also implies that the family is the "adjusting" system—it is the one which has to shift, change, and somehow make do the best way it can. We have taken these assumptions for granted, but yet we have not always considered them in social action or development programs. Along with other recipients of the social consequences of technological and scientific advancement and change, the family has assumed its share of "benign neglect." Yet, despite severe stresses and shifts in structure and function, the family has survived dire predictions to the contrary which seem to rise every so often in both scholarly and popular thinking.

It has become commonplace in many disciplines and applied fields today to use a systems approach to analysis of phenomena. Overuse sometimes leads to oversimplification; however, despite this danger I will use a systems approach to some extent in this chapter because it seems a fruitful one for examining the relationship between the community system and the family system. The notion of adjustment also fits this model because it implies that a change in one system necessarily calls for change in another system. Though "adjustment" is a suitable term and does imply some kind of change, it also carries the connotation of returning to a prior condition or achieving a state of stability. Therefore, I would like to broaden the meaning of the more traditional use of adjustment to include *adapting* and *coping*. It may be splitting hairs to suggest there is a difference, but

MARGARET J. BUBOLZ is Professor, Department of Family and Child Sciences, Michigan State University.

54

I think these terms imply more flexibility and creativity to meet new conditions and more dynamic action than adjustment. In addition, adapting also implies change in both structure and function. Hence, whenever I use the term adjustment I will be using it in this broader sense.

This chapter will be largely speculative, rather than factual or hard data oriented. I will be drawing upon previous research and observation related to families and family response to crises and social change. I will suggest a model for viewing family response to community decline, and I will indicate some of the areas where we might expect change and adaption in families in declining communities. But first I will discuss briefly the reciprocal relationships and interactions between family and community, as a background for a closer analysis of the internal family system.

We often look at the family as the receiver and adjuster to change in other systems; sometimes the family has been referred to as a sponge absorbing from the outside. It has been suggested that this sponge-like, or adaptive function, is the most important function of the family in contemporary society. In reality the family and other systems are mutually interdependent. From an economic standpoint the community furnishes wages, goods, and services, but the family contributes labor and private capital to the economy. It also helps develop and sustain motivation to contribute these. The community helps give individuals identity and status and support, but the family shapes and creates the community through its participation and involvement and sharing of resources—or conversely, it may fail in this function. An important function of the family for society is socialization of children and youth in the major values of the community and for future roles in the community, work, and in the family. Another significant function of the family is to help provide emotional support and release from stresses experienced in the larger society, so that individuals can return to "the outside" to play social roles. It is this function which many believe is a primary one today, both for the individual and society, and one which may contribute to internal family stresses, resulting in instability and disorganization. The stresses that are present in declining communities—unemployment, poverty, lack of adequate community supports, and services such as health, educational, and recreational facilities—come home to the family and in turn feed back into the community.

It is not my purpose to discuss community decline, but a working definition of the community variable is needed in order to consider the family variable. I consider declining communities to be those which have: (1) declining numbers of people; (2) a diminishing economic base; (3) probably fewer or less diverse or responsive social and economic institutions, and (4) lessening opportunities for attainment of a richer life.

There are many kinds and sizes of communities experiencing population decline. A 1963 study by Beegle, Marshall, and Rice of "County Migration Patterns in the North Central States," for 1940, 1950, and 1960 [2] indicated that a large portion of the counties in which there was a net out-migration had one of two basic patterns related to farm operator family level of living and employment in manufacturing. One large group of counties had a low level of living and low employment in manufacturing; the other large group had a high level of living and low employment in manufacturing. There were heavy concentrations of counties with low levels of living in northern Michigan, Wisconsin, Minnesota and southern Ohio, Indiana, Illinois and Missouri, southeastern Kansas, as well as some counties in Nebraska and North and South Dakota. The counties with high levels of living were found in large portions of the Corn and Wheat Belts in Indiana, Illinois, Iowa, southern Minnesota, Kansas, Nebraska, and parts of North and South Dakota. Study of family adjustment to community decline would have to consider the nature of the community and the nature of the decline. This could be a fruitful area for research, to see if there are differences in family adaptation patterns in different kinds of declining communities.

Data reported for use by the Committee on Agriculture and Forestry of the United States Senate in 1972 [29] described characteristics of U.S. rural areas with noncommuting populations. They indicated that a little more than half of all towns in the counties defined in this way (counties beyond the observed commuting fields) showed declines in population. This condition occurred predominantly among towns of less than 500 population, fully 60 percent of which declined between 1960 and 1970. Size of community would thus be another important variable. Very small communities, the most common kind, would not have a sufficient population base to support economic and social organizations and public agencies, which would in turn influence family adaptation patterns and alternatives. The age and sex structure of the population that stays, as well as the population that leaves, would also have significant implications for family life.

Since it is not my purpose to analyze the declining community, I will not pursue the matters I have raised further except to indicate that these issues, as well as others related to the community, need to be kept in mind as one considers family adaptation.

FAMILY ADAPTATION AND RESPONSE TO DECLINE. It would be desirable to be able to present a model or description of family response to community decline based on research findings or on a well thought out theoretical framework. But there are relatively few studies that have dealt with the behavior of the whole family system in relation to its changing social-psychological milieu. We are dealing essentially with a process that occurs over time, almost imperceptibly, unless a crisis event triggers dramatic changes.

The example we had of the Loud family, observed, photographed, and recorded for seven months, then shown to the nation via educational TV in 1973, illustrated this process. It indicated how seemingly little went on that was of importance in the daily activities and conversations—certainly on the surface it was not as exciting and dramatic as the soap opera accounts of family life—but eventually something did happen; things had changed. This is one of few naturalistic observations of this process of change in social-psychological family environment.

We can, however, look to related research and what we know about family groups and suggest some of the internal responses which may occur—and why they may be different for different families. Earlier generations of social scientists paid attention to family response to such crises as unemployment, war separation, death, and illness. I am borrowing from some of this earlier work and have modified a model for viewing families in crisis which I think may be useful in viewing families and what happens in communities where opportunities and life chances are diminishing and in which there are crises for some families.

The essential parts of this model are:

Community Conditions or Situations
>   For example, loss of a job; closing down of a business, community facility, or service; moving away of family members and/or relatives and friends.

Impingement on the Family in terms of:
>   Organization and Structure
>>   Size, composition, life cycle stage, age and sex structure.
>>   Role allocation, division of labor, who has the most power in certain decisions and areas of life.
>>   Emotional climate and structure—who gives emotional support and affection to whom?
>   Goals: Values
>>   Economic security, health, education, as well as a variety of more specific values and goals; may or may not be clearly and explicitly formulated.
>   Resources
>>   Material goods and assets.
>>   Personal: health, skills, abilities, "inner strengths."
>>   Social: relatives, friends, neighbors.

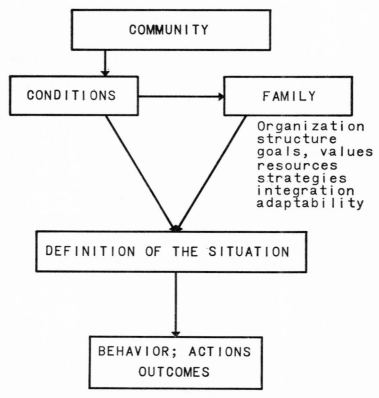

FIG. 5.1. Interrelationships of family and community.

Community supports and services and people's perceptions
of them as valid and accessible for them.

Position and status in the community.

Strategies

Techniques for solving problems, for coping, for managing
and using resources.

Past history and experience in solving problems.

Integration

The bonds of coherence and unity running through family
life including common interests, values and goals, mutual support and cooperation, affection and a sense of
economic and emotional interdependence.

Adaptability

Coping capacity, ability to shift courses, change goals, shift roles, use the leadership ideas and skills of more than one person.[1]

The conditions impinging on the family combined with their internal organization, goals, values, resources, strategies, and capacities unite to produce the following:

The Definition of the Situation. This may be considered to be of three kinds:

    Objective: That of outsiders, researchers, extension or development agents. May be factual, statistical, and in some respects "true."

    Cultural: That of the community in their terms, based on their values and perceptions.

    Subjective: The family's own definition from the standpoint of their values, goals, position, resources, and the perceptions of the alternatives known and open to them.[2]

Following on the definition of the situation are the behaviors and actions taken:

The Outcomes or Consequences
    Decisions made, actions taken or not taken, etc.
    Outcomes in terms of stability, reorganization, restructuring, breakdown, etc.

    I believe that this model, admittedly oversimplified and not fully developed, offers possibilities for research and action programs and provides a framework for understanding differences and similarities among families we may be studying or working with, and the kinds of adaptations they can or may make. This model can also give us clues of where intervention into the system could be most feasible or fruitful, and some insight into the kinds of support systems which may need to be established and where information is needed.

    An example illustrating support systems is drawn from my experience in the Cooperative Extension Service in the Upper Peninsula of Michigan, an area which had experienced considerable decline when I worked there. I was always struck by the qualitative differ-

    1. Angell's study, *The Family Encounters the Depression* [1], found that adaptation was the most important factor in a family's successful coping with crises related to the depression. He also found that families who had higher material goals and more concern about status and position were less able to adapt than those with fewer material goals and less concern about status.
    2. The theorem of W. I. Thomas: that "If men define situations as real they are real in their consequences," applies here.

ences which seemed to exist among the people in the various areas and counties. When I worked in Chippewa County at the eastern end of the peninsula, a county which had had a net migration of nearly 20 percent from 1960 to 1970, I noticed the feeling of apathy, little willingness to become involved in community activities, or to take part in things which could benefit them. On the other hand, when I was in western Michigan which in the same period had experienced similar population decline (e.g., Gogebic, which had had nearly a 15 percent net out-migration, and Iron, which had close to 20 percent out-migration), I did not sense this same feeling. There was much greater participation in activities, many demands upon the extension service and other agencies for development efforts, and a feeling of vitality. I wondered what made the difference.

No doubt there were many variables involved such as the nature and quality of leadership and differences in the objective conditions of decline, but I also believe some of the differences were in the emotional and support systems of the families. There was evidence of more extended family relationships and kinship support systems and ethnic enclaves in these two counties. Old country customs and traditions survived; feelings of pride in one's heritage were maintained through festivals, religious groups, and radio and television programs. I am not espousing a return to ethnocentrism or group rivalry, but I am suggesting that attention again be given to the strengths which come from pride in oneself, seen as part of a group in which one has pride. This can help give feelings of control of one's destiny and a more positive self-concept and identity, as well as provide mutually supportive emotional and social relationships.

This observation and considerable research dispel the notion that the dominant American family type is the isolated nuclear family described by Talcott Parsons. To be sure, the nuclear family in the sense of parents and their children in one household is the most common form, and in increasing numbers it is often a one-parent family, with children sometimes shared or passed between parents. However, isolation of the family from extended kin is not as widespread as once assumed, and even though family members move, contacts are maintained and help is exchanged. For example, a study of rural-to-urban migrants in Kentucky demonstrated that the presence of relatives in the recipient community, for emotional support as well as practical information about jobs, etc., was an important factor in adjustment to the new community.

The nature of support and relationships with the extended family are often decisive factors in a family's adaptations and decisions in response to community change or decline. The flow back of help and information from those who leave is also an important element in a family's adaptation. In this respect the age and other characteristics of those who migrate in contrast to those who stay are important variables for consideration.

Research in the 1930s and 1940s indicated that rural migrants were selected from the younger age groups, with females somewhat more likely to migrate and at earlier ages than males. Those who migrated tended to receive more formal education. The age differential probably still exists, but the very rapid decrease in number of farms in the last generation has affected the migration rate among all age groups, males and females.

Poverty. From the standpoint of effects on families of declining economic conditions, the result of poverty on human lives is surely the most inclusive, devastating, and degrading. Poor nutrition and health; inadequate housing; lack of access to good educational, recreational, medical, and social services; plus the debilitating effects of lack of hope for improvement are typical conditions associated with the lives of poor people. The Report of the President's National Advisory Commission on Rural Poverty, *The People Left Behind* [28], indicated that in 1967 over 14 million rural Americans lived in poverty. At that time 40 percent of the nation's poor lived in rural areas, even though only 30 percent of the total U.S. population lived in rural America. The poor in the declining small towns of our country, off the superhighways and out of sight, are today's "invisible poor."

Life Cycle Stage. Viewing the family and the individuals in it from a developmental point of view, going through various stages beginning with marriage, through childbearing, rearing, children leaving home, the middle and older years, through retirement, and death of spouses is a useful framework for describing the typical tasks and problems which families in similar stages will encounter. It can also help in assessing the kinds of adaptations and changes families can make. In order to assess a community's needs and resources, and to design development programs for the community and its families, it is important to know the population profiles by life cycle stages. For example, declining rural communities often have disproportionate numbers of older people, and many single older women (since women have a longer life expectancy and in the later years outnumber men by 3- or 4-to-1). Health, educational, recreational, employment, and other facilities will need to be adapted to fit the particular people of a given community.

From the standpoint of adaptability of families and their capacity to cope with changes and crises, some interesting differences between three adult generations of the same families in regard to help and support patterns and decision making were found by Reuben Hill [15, 24] and his associates at the University of Minnesota. The middle generation (parent generation) gave help in both directions, to their married children and to their parents; they received markedly less than they gave. The young-couple generation (child) mainly needed and received help in areas of child care and financial assistance. The older generation (grandparent) was especially in need of assistance with illness, household management, and emotional gratification. This generation received more help than it gave, with the young generation being more nearly in balance in its giving and receiving.

In regard to decision making, the youngest generation did the most planning, the oldest the least. The youngest was most likely to be definite in setting a date for taking action and to have a longer view in planning; the grandparent generation was most often indefinite. Definite plans in all generations were more likely to be carried out, the short-run more than long-run. The grandparent generation made the fewest plans and took the fewest actions but fulfilled the highest proportion of its plans. The parent generation showed a moderate number of plans but fulfilled the lowest proportion. The majority of changes completed by all three generations were not planned in advance. The youngest generation did more rational decision making in terms of searching for information, weighing alternatives, and taking into account long-term as well as short-term consequences before taking action.

These findings suggest many implications for family adaptation and response to alternative courses of action which might be posed.

Role Relationships, Assignments, and Power Relations. These are dimensions of family structure which will influence adaptation, and which also may shift in response to community change. For instance, in some declining rural communities there may be both need and opportunity for more women to enter the work force. Previous research has indicated that family task and decision making patterns are related to employment status of the wife, with a trend toward more sharing of household tasks and decision making when wives go to work. Some research has suggested that wives enhance their power vis-a-vis their husbands when they are employed and have more resources at their command. However, employment must be seen as interacting with the existing family ideology regarding man-woman relations, status and power, and the personalities of those involved.

Research on rural and urban differences in husband-wife involvement in decision making has shown no significant differences which can be attributed to rural or urban residence. Any discernible differences were more related to socioeconomic class. Lower class families have been found to have more rigid role allocation and differentiation of the sexes in household tasks and social activities along traditional sex-role lines, and less equalitarian and shared decision making.

However, rural-urban differences have been found in marital satisfaction, with rural women expressing lower levels of marital and personal satisfaction. On the other hand, up to now at least, there has been greater marital stability and lower divorce rates among rural couples. Increased employment of rural wives with related increase in resources and power—coupled with widespread trends toward more equality in relationships among many heretofore subservient groups —may result in the unanticipated consequence of lessened family stability and increased rates of dissolution among some families in their adaptations to community change and decline.

This leads me to suggest some other longer-term outcomes for individuals and the society at large as a result of social change manifested in community decline.

Contrary to the suggestion that the family has lost a major role in the educational process, I assert that socialization of children, youth, and also of adults, in values, goals, attitudes, habits, and social roles is a primary function of families. Considerable research has indicated that families are important sources of these socialization outcomes not only for young children but for youths as well. Of particular importance is socialization for competence, for the feeling that one has control over one's life, for a positive self-image, for adaptability and flexibility, and for willingness to take risks and chances.

It makes a great deal of difference to not only the individuals involved, but to the rest of us as well, whether or not the socialization processes going on in the family, as well as in the community, are contributing to the development of competent persons who can cope with the vicissitudes of contemporary life and provide the kinds of leadership and citizens a society needs. Support of quality education programs at all levels becomes difficult in declining communities when the resource base is diminishing. It becomes all the more important, however, that investment in such programs as Head Start; family life groups; parent education and enrichment programs; day care; and other education efforts become our primary development goals. Investment in *family development* as well as in *economic development* must be a part of rural development. I also would like to elaborate on the model presented earlier. I propose that a cybernetic model is needed to take into account the mutual effects of systems on each other, the feedback of actions and consequences in one system on the other, and vice versa. K. Dean Black [5] suggests that human systems can adapt by not only making preprogrammed responses, but by generating new structures, new responses, new behaviors, and making new operations. This process is called *morphogenesis*. He further suggests that a cybernetic-morphogenic model for study and analysis of family behavior would be most fruitful for conceptualizing many problems researchers and change agents are concerned about. However, at present few are developed.

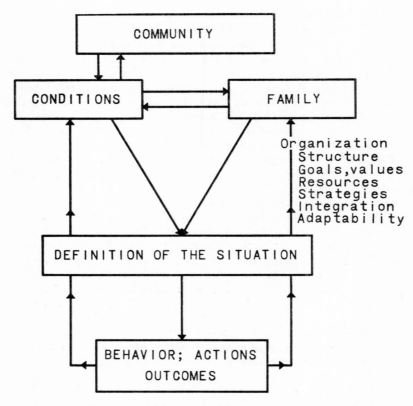

FIG. 5.2. Feedback model of interaction of family and community.

I do not have a fully developed model by any means but would like to suggest that basic elements include two subsystems, Community and Family, along with definitions of their situations, and the behaviors and actions taken by the family and the community, leading to various outcomes. Actions taken by the family feed back into it as well as into the community; likewise community actions have repercussions on the community and the families in it. If the actions (or nonactions) taken by the family make the conditions worse, a vicious cycle is the result; the situation worsens. The same can be true for community action. However, if the actions taken by either system change the conditions for the better, the vicious cycle can be broken. In rural development efforts in declining communities, the feedback processes and probable effects on families of decisions and actions taken with regard to economic organizations, community services, etc., must be taken into account. The goal should be to make both the community and families morphogenic, and more creatively adaptive in dealing with recurring human problems.

REFERENCES

1. Angell, R. C. 1936. *The family encounters the depression*. New York: Scribner's.
2. Beegle, A., Marshall, D., and Rice, R. 1963. Selected factors related to county migration patterns in the north central states, 1940–50 and 1950–60. East Lansing: Michigan State University Agricultural Experiment Station, North Central Regional Research Publication 147.
3. Beegle, J. A. 1971. Population growth and redistribution. East Lansing: Michigan State University Agricultural Experiment Station, Research Report 150.
4. Bell, Norman, and Vogel, E. 1968. *A modern introduction to the family*. New York: Free Press.
5. Black, K. D., and Broderick, C. B. 1972. Systems theory vs. reality. Paper presented at National Council on Family Relations Annual Meeting October 1972, Portland, Oregon.
6. Blood, R., and Wolfe, D. 1960. *Husbands and wives*. New York: Free Press.
7. Bultena, G., and Marshall, D. 1970. Family patterns of migrant and nonmigrant retirees. *J. Marriage and Fam.* 32(1 Feb.): 89–93.
8. Burchinal, L., and Bauder, W. 1965. Decision-making and role patterns among Iowa farm and nonfarm families. *J. Marriage and Fam.* 27(4 Nov.): 525–32.
9. Center for Agricultural and Rural Development. 1972. *Seminar papers*. Rural Community Development Seminar, Jan.–May 1972, Iowa State University.
10. Copp, J., ed. 1964. *Our changing rural society: perspectives and trends*. Ames: Iowa State Univ Press.
11. Farson, R., Hauser, P., Stroup, H., and Wiener, A. 1969. *The future of the family*. New York: Family Service Association of America.
12. Ferman, Louis A., et al. 1966. *Poverty in America*. Ann Arbor: Univ. of Michigan Press.
13. Glasser, Paul H., and Glasser, Lois M. 1970. *Families in crisis*. New York: Harper and Row.
14. Goode, W. 1963. *World revolution and family patterns*. New York: Free Press.
15. Hill, Reuben. 1949. *Families under stress*. New York: Harper and Brothers.
16. Iowa State University, College of Home Economics. 1972. *Families of the future*. Ames: Iowa State Univ. Press.
17. Komarovsky, Mirra. 1940. *The unemployed man and his family*. New York: Dryden Press.
18. Landis, J., and Stoetzer, L. 1966. An exploratory study of middle-class migrant families. *J. Marriage and Fam.* 28(4 Nov.): 51–53.
19. Nimkoff, M. F. 1965. *Comparative family systems*. Boston: Houghton Mifflin.
20. Schwarzweller, H. 1964. Parental family ties and social integration of rural to urban migrants. *J. Marriage and Fam.* 26(4 Nov.): 410–16.

21. Schwarzweller, H., and Seggar, J. 1967. Kinship involvement: A factor in the adjustment of rural migrants. *J. Marriage and Fam.* 29(4 Nov.): 662–71.
22. Shanas, E., and Streib, G. 1965. *Social structure and the family: Generational relations* (esp. parts 1–4). Englewood Cliffs, N.J.: Prentice-Hall.
23. Skolnick, A., and Skolnick, J. 1971. *Family in transition.* Boston: Little, Brown and Co.
24. Sussman, M. 1968. *Sourcebook on marriage and the family,* 3rd ed. Boston: Houghton Mifflin.
25. United States Department of Agriculture, Economic Research Service. 1969. U.S. population mobility and distribution, charts on recent trends. E.R.S. Report 436. Washington, D.C.
26. ———. 1968. A national program of research for rural development and family living. Prepared by a Joint Task Force of U.S.D.A. and the State Universities and Land Grant Colleges, November 1968.
27. United States Government Printing Office. 1970. *A new life for the country.* Report of the President's Task Force on Rural Development. Washington, D.C.
28. ———. 1967. *The people left behind.* Report by the President's National Commission on Rural Poverty. Washington, D.C.
29. United States Senate, Committee on Agriculture and Forestry. 1972. *Characteristics of U.S. rural areas with non-commuting population.* Washington, D.C.: U.S. Government Printing Office.
30. Vincent, C. E. 1966. Familia spongia: The adaptive function. *J. Marriage and Fam.* 28(1 Feb.): 29–36.
31. Young, R., and Larson, O. 1970. Social ecology of a rural community. *Rural Soc.* 35(3 Sept.): 337–53.

CHAPTER SIX

CONSEQUENCES FOR LEADERSHIP
AND PARTICIPATION

EUGENE C. ERICKSON

CONCERN WITH problems caused by the decline in rural (and agricultural) villages is not a recent phenomenon. In 1911, John Gillette [15] stated, ". . . the most serious consideration in the shift of population from country to city is involved in the loss of leadership sustained by rural communities." Wilson Gee [14] reached a similar conclusion in "A Qualitative Study of Rural Population in a Single Township," published in 1933. He cites a "severe depletion" in the rural township's upper class during the 30-year period from 1900 to 1930 and concludes, "This large loss of the leading stock of the community . . . must . . . undesirably lower the levels of life in the rural section affected."

Congressional action is one indication that rural development may continue to be a subject for concern, analysis, and discussion for some time to come.

Sweeping changes in the distribution of people, in the services available to them, and in the overall quality of life have been occurring in both the private and public sectors of U.S. society since the onslaught of industrialization at the end of the nineteenth century. Of particular significance to rural areas has been the shifting from informal institutions to formal organizations centralized in urban centers. Few people would lament many of the changes that have occurred. Mechanization has notably reduced the physical drudgery in our lives. The revolution from the limitations imposed by the horse and buggy and the dirt road is hardly one any administration today would try to reverse.

EUGENE C. ERICKSON is Associate Professor of Rural Sociology, Cornell University.

But there have been losses too. In this chapter I will explore what these sweeping changes imply for the declining small community. To do this, I shall give an overview of some historical events; look briefly at the structural relationships between decline and other variables as they are currently known; develop, in a speculative way, the implications for policy making or leadership in such localities; and deal with ideas that lend themselves to further study.

HISTORICAL CHANGE. It is doubtful that U.S. communities were ever completely independent. They probably came closest in the latter part of the seventeenth century when craftsmen had learned to use native materials, leadership had arisen in somewhat stable form, and socialization had been institutionalized. Until the end of the nineteenth century, communities continued to be relatively autonomous. Most food and services were produced locally. This was the case in even the eastern communities which were subjected to extensive out-migration all during the period of settlement of the frontier [8]. The construction of roads, canals, and railways as well as the movement of people in and out of communities all over the country did develop some linkages so that the self-sufficiency or autonomy was only relative.

During nearly all of that century, technology was adapted to the environment. Farm families—and they were large families—supplied an adequate labor force. Horses permitted the exploitation of much marginal land. When technological advances hit the farming sector in the early part of the twentieth century, changes came with a vengeance. Farms increased in size, and marginal farms were dropped out of production or the basis of production was shifted. This process continued into the 1960s and 70s.

The informal relationships that give identity to a neighborhood or community have changed just as drastically—even if less obviously. In periods such as the nineteenth century when transportation technology sharply limited distances traveled, the neighborhood or the small community was a very real unit with a definable territory. To say it was a unit suggests that the norms and values existing among the residents had a significant binding effect upon the people. There is much sociological literature supporting the principle that frequency of interaction affects the formation and functioning of a system. Also, the family, being larger than today's and more dependent on itself, was a significant small unit within the community system.

The literature is sparse, but I suspect the social class distinctions that have so divided twentieth century America were less sharply drawn up to the time of the rise of the great corporations. The disparities in family wealth were possibly no greater in the nineteenth century than they are in the twentieth. The estates of the Rockefellers, Harrimans, and many others existed to be sure, but this fact is more significant for what it tells about the distribution of resources and separation of classes overall than for what light it throws on the vast majority of communities. Away from those great estates on the Hudson and the large plantations in the South[1] there were the places where the vast majority of people lived, and it is with these communities that we are concerned.

Surely, classes existed in these communities too, and wealth was by no means shared proportionally. Yet, in spite of the disproportionate distribution of resources, it is my contention that being "of" a neighborhood implied a reciprocal obligation among its members for mutual support functions. Examples are the barn-raisings and house-warmings. These were more than an earlier form of social security; they were also a means of information exchange, and by setting the standards of acceptable behavior, they were a means of social control.

We can best understand leadership systems in such communities in the context of historical patterns. First we should recall that both an informal and a formal (or political) system existed. In the informal system persons were valued for their judgment, and in the formal system they were elected to offices such as town board member, mayor, or city councilman. "Highly respected" (elite) people were sent to the legislature and other state offices. During the nineteenth century and well into the twentieth, the formal and informal leadership systems were closely intertwined. People were assigned leadership roles; that is, they were respected and trusted in their judgments concerning policies because they reflected the normative system out of which they arose.

William Seward was a lawyer in the small city of Auburn, New York, but he served as governor twice and later was secretary of state. Yet, his ties to Auburn remained strong throughout his life [6]. In my new hometown of Ithaca, New York, in the third quarter of the nineteenth century Ezra Cornell was a businessman who served on a variety of local boards and also in the state legislature [4]. This pattern of local entrepreneurs holding public office continued well into the present century. But by the mid-twentieth century the persons judged influential were not usually the occupants of formal government positions (though at one time in their lives many had been

1. It is difficult to say whether the incidence of "estates" was a purely regional phenomenon. The plantation system permeated the South, but estates existed in the Northeast and in the Great Plains. Shortly after the initial settlement, there were vast "corporate farms" on the plains. Presumably the technology and the system of management were not sufficiently advanced to sustain these farms, and many, like the plantations of the South, were soon dismembered.

occupants of these positions) [2,37,38]. In the small town the man elected to the town board was, it appears, a "respected," as well as political, individual. He was close to his constituency physically and probably psychologically.

I would make the further assertion that where the political office-holder, the respected community leader, and indeed the neighbor was one and the same person, his role as officeholder was extremely diffuse. There is an account of a man making a request of the chairman of the town board in a rural area in North Dakota. The man said, "Oscar, since you are chairman of the town board, I'd like to borrow your violin to play at the dance on Saturday night." The official shook his head in wonder but loaned the violin. This same official took people to the doctor and performed other services far beyond the formally stated requirements of a town board member. What distinguishes this officeholder is a strong element of paternalism, and the term is not used negatively. Relationships were probably such that the needs of people were cared for.

A corollary to this thesis [34] concerns the extent to which an individual's personal liberty was affected by such pervasive personal relationships. It can be argued plausibly that these close-knit communities were extremely constraining. Particularly, we should be careful not to assign the "Golden Age Syndrome" to rural life. It has been suggested that few among us would care to return to the "technological drudgery" of earlier times. Similarly, most would not, I suspect, like to return to the oppressive control by an elitist leadership system. Still, in our attempt to create the conditions for a "better life" by turning most tasks over to machines and by giving up direct control by our neighbors, we run the risk of severe personal alienation.

Historical Coda. In 1911 Gillette [15] was concerned with the "conspicuous dearth of leadership" in rural life. He conducted a study of a number of students of normal schools and colleges who returned to the rural setting. In his words, "The indications are that relatively few . . . either of those who came from rural regions or otherwise, enter into country life." He goes on to say that the agricultural class is "almost without leadership in the sphere of political life and must depend on representatives of other classes to secure justice." Gillette was still making the same point 18 years later [16]. It was leadership loss that Gee [14] lamented in 1933. And in a 1940 study of agricultural villages, Jenkins [23] deplored the "weeding out of leaders in the middle-aged and youth groups."

Mather [28] and later Anderson [1] developed the more significant implications of these rural population losses. From studies in the 1930s and 40s, both observed the marked reduction of participation in associations. This dispersal of association patterns further tore away at the fabric of community life. A 1965 study by O'Shea and Gray [31], based on a National Opinion Research Center national sample shows that participation in community affairs was closely related to income. Whereas only 4 percent of the respondents called themselves "leaders," 76 percent classified themselves as "ordinary citizens" or "not a part of the community at all."

We are all aware of the ever increasing centralization of services, retail businesses, voluntary associations, and government and education facilities [5, 20, 27, 29]. The change in school districts—which comprise one structural access people have to membership—is illustrative. The number of school districts in the state of New York, for example, dropped from about 11,000 in 1845, to 1,465 in 1950, to 772 in 1972. To be even more specific, the rural central school my own children attend is a composite of 12 former districts. Regardless of the value of such centralization, the point is that one more structure has been lost. As a result, some people at least have become "marginal" in their relationships to the dominant society [12].

STRUCTURAL RELATIONSHIPS WITH DECLINE. In order to obtain a better feeling for the conditions within declining communities, I examined changes in population within the last three decades in 300 counties in the 12 Northeastern states and the District of Columbia. I then related population change to a variety of institutional characteristics,[2] selecting variables that give clues to the demographic structure of the county, its educational level, the business structure, the communications patterns, its economic resources, and its government structure.

I have made a similar comparison for the 62 New York counties and for the 134 "Hinterland" counties in the Northeastern area. ("Hinterland" refers to essentially rural areas without a major trading center of 10,000 or more people. Hinterland, Basic Trading Center, Suburban, and Major Center or Metropolitan are county classifications derived from an index of business, manufacturing, and newspaper data. See Eberts and Kluess [11].) My reasons for using Northeastern state data were that much of this is based on specifically constructed scales or secondary sources other than the census, and it was convenient. Before any final determination can be made of the applicability of these results to other areas, further study is obviously in order.

2. I wish to thank the organizers and sponsors of the New York State Data Bank—which is composed largely of data for the concepts of the CSRS-NE-47 Project, under the guidance of Paul Eberts and Fred Schmidt—for permitting access to the information and particularly to Mr. Frank E. Mattson for compiling the statistics, and to my colleague, Professor Dan Moore, for conversations about them. For more detail on the NE-47 Project, see Eberts [10].

TABLE 6.1. Personian correlation coefficients between specified variables and percent population change over certain decades for 300 counties in the 12 northeastern states and the District of Columbia

Variables	Percent of Population Change Between		
	1940–1950	1950–1960	1960–1970
		(r)	
Percent of population aged 65 and over			
1950	—.38†		
1960		—.47†	
Median age of population			
1950	.01		
1960		—.13*	
Percent of population classified urban			
1950	.27†		
1960		.36†	
Median school years completed			
1950	.37†		
1960		.53†	
Percent of population over 25 years with 5 years or less of education			
1950	—.21†		
1960		—.33†	
Median income			
1950	.57†		
1960		.69†	
Percent of families with incomes less than			
$2000 in 1950	—.49†		
$3000 in 1960		—.60†	
Number of manufacturing units			
1953	.09		
1958		.09	
1963			.01
Dun and Bradstreet scale			
1963	.16†		
1960		.11*	
1970			.10*
Total per capita expenditures			
1957		.16†	
1966			.32†
Number of people eligible to vote who voted			
1950	—.09		
1960		—.23†	
1968			—.27†

SOURCE: New York State Data Bank.
* Significant at .05.
† Significant at .01.

Demographic. Among the 300 Northeastern counties there was a very high negative correlation between the percentage of population increase and the proportion of the population over 65 years of age. This was true of both the 1940–1950 decade and the 1950–1960 decade. Though we did not check each county, it is probable that the counties being considered had a high out-migration. The median age of the population was less clearly associated. It did not correlate with growth in the 1940s, and there was a negative correlation in the 1950s. The proportion of the population that was classified as urban was also compared to the growth variable. As the urban proportion of the county increased, there was a definite tendency toward increase in the rate of growth. Thus, the more isolated, the more hinterland, the more rural the county, the smaller the increase in population and the greater the probability of a declining population. (See Table 6.1 for the specific correlation coefficients.)

Education. There also was a very high positive correlation between the percent population increase and the median number of school years completed in both the 1940s and 1950s. Similarly, there was a negative correlation between the growth variable and the proportion of persons over 25 years of age who had less than 5 years of education.

Economic Resources. Family income is often taken as an indication to some degree of economic resources in an area. Again, over the 300 counties, median family income was very highly correlated with population growth in both the 1940s and 50s. The low income factor, i.e., the proportion of persons with incomes below an arbitrary poverty figure ($2,000 in 1950, $3,000 in 1960), was very clearly negatively correlated with the growth variable in both the 1940s and 50s.

The extent of business activity in the area was also observed. The total number of manufacturing establishments was compared to the growth variable; there was no relationship. A scale from Dunn and Bradstreet reports, which indicates the range of activity in businesses varying from gas stations to a news syndicate, was developed, and for this measure there is a relationship with growth in all three decades.

Leadership Systems. Of particular interest is the viability of the governmental decision apparatus in a county. Unfortunately, at this time we have little hard data on government organization. We do have the per capita expenditures for all government services (education, highways, public welfare, hospitals, health, and police) for each of the 300 counties. In the decade of the 1950s there was a correlation between this factor and the population growth variable, and the relationship held in the decade of the 1960s. Thus, the greater the population growth, the more the expenditure of government resources.

When the growth variable was compared to voting patterns, however, the relationship did not hold in the 1940s, and was negatively correlated in both the 1950s and 60s. Thus, the greater the population change, the higher the proportion of persons who were eligible to vote who did not vote. Eberts [10] maintains that this is a transitory finding associated with high rates of migration; that when people first move into an area they are effectively disenfranchised.

A summary statement of the discussion to this point is that generally, aged and rural populations with lower than normal education, already low income, and relatively fewer economic resources upon which to draw are faced with further decline relative to other areas.

An Illinois study [18] notes that there are places without services now and without the resources to establish services which might draw more people to the area. Replacing just one school building for a moderate size school population can easily cost several million dollars. Government services cost a great deal of money. Voluntary services are costly in time and effort and may depend on access to the information as a basis for their organization and delivery. Such access may be limited by the generally low level of education.

IMPLICATIONS FOR POLITICAL CHANGES. We now turn to the broader question of what these data (and ideas) seem to indicate for the organization of political systems. First we will review the constraints to the specific political conditions posed here. The historical argument can be summarized as saying that in communities with constraints imposed by technology, including transportation technology, there tended to be a greater intensity of interaction. Also, interaction networks tended to center around individuals and families within the community.

Those who occupied leadership roles within this system could more truly represent their constituency. These leaders, both public and private, both formal and informal, might well have been those persons who also directly controlled other resources. They were owners and operators of economic firms and at the same time councilmen in the political structures. The class structure, such as it was, might well have led to a relatively smooth operation of the system as well as tight concise control by an elite. The changes in social organization, especially those changes that gave individuals a greater range of options (one of which was to leave the community), were surely most dramatic where, with growing industrialization, the relationships external to the community came to control it. The external control of manufacturing, mining, and marketing had extensive effects. Illustrative is the conflict between the populists and the "eastern bankers" in the 1920s and 30s.

Even as the decisions concerning resource allocation were removed from the locality, other decisions remained local and local government still functioned. Presumably, there was a shift in leadership within the formal government structure to persons who represented a different constituency. Rather than by neighborhood, the new constituency tends to be defined on a more segmented basis: political ideology, occupation, interest group, or the like.

Literature in recent years seems to indicate that power is derived largely—but not entirely—from valuations made in the social relationship. This means that the normative definitions in a system define the form of the allocations of "social goods," which in turn form the basis of policy making [41]. Numerous classifications of these normative conditions are possible, but a useful one has been developed by Linton Freeman and his colleagues [13]. Their classification—derived from factor analysis of leaders—is shown as follows:

Classification	Illustrative Items[3]
Social Level–Social Class Membership	Education Occupation Income Political Identification Father's Education
Division of Labor	Sex Characteristics Occupation
Life Cycle–Stages of Social Development	Age Marital Status Home Ownership
Family Social Level	Father's Occupation Father's Education
Ethnic Status	Religious Affiliation Ethnic Background Political Identification
Localism	Place of Birth Length of Residence Orientation to Community Number of Years with Firm Father's Birthplace

A study [22] made as early as 1928 showed that the leaders in village communities had some of these same characteristics: 73 percent had lived in the communities more than 25 years, 63 percent were owners or managers. These patterns have not changed. Or have they? Surely there is some kind of dynamic occurring in a large number of community settings. Some social scientists have found what they argue is a pluralistic structure of power in the community. While those who hold seats in government in a pluralistic structure may

3. These items include those of Freeman, et al., and others added by other research.

have the same characteristics as those who do not occupy offices, this is unlikely. It is unlikely because they are presumed, as their actions seem to indicate, to "represent"—if you please—distinctly different sectors of the community. As men from different sectors of the community come together, for whatever reasons, a different dynamic must surely occur in their interaction. I would expect them to be oriented more to the task, and especially the outcome, than to the rules of the game or the process.

From a very different research source a similar idea is drawn. Robert Crain and Donald Rosenthal [7] found that communities with higher levels of education and with a greater number of organizations had significantly greater participation in public decision making.

In the Northeast, the structural conditions associated with decline included an aging population, relatively less exposure to schools and classrooms, relatively lower incomes (and, presumably, poorer access to the jobs that are sources of information). This is supported by a study of town board and town planning board members in a rural county in upstate New York [40]. When these towns were classified on a developing-declining scale, the declining towns were those with long-term residents occupying seats of control and without planning boards. (The town boards held decision making "close to the chest.") Even when the towns classified as "stable" (i.e., not developing appreciably) had planning boards, the influence of the planning boards was negligible.

Participation. The outline being drawn is one in which development—
    whether it is defined as increasing population, increasing the tax
    base, or increasing the number of decisions that are brought forward for public scrutiny—seems to be closely related to something vaguely called participation. The argument suggests that it is this participation, this access to those loci in which public decisions that affect all our lives are made, that has eroded over the last 40 to 50 years.

I wish to guard against misinterpretation of this argument. It is all too easy to lament the passing of these "nice homogeneous communities" and neighborhoods. No return to those communities of the past is possible; the technological and environmental elements that surrounded them are gone. It is even unlikely many would wish to duplicate the more constraining aspects of social life of the past. Let me underscore a corollary idea that any reconstruction of neighborhoods must consider not only the elements of modern technology but the nature of the social interactions we wish to foster. I am impressed by the attempts of innovators such as Peter Goldmark [17] who are experimenting with the creation of new rural societies by using the most modern of telecommunications techniques. Much more needs to be done to specify the quality of the social world to which we wish individuals to have access.

We turn finally to the practical issue of models of participation. To review the burgeoning literature on participation is at the same time exhilarating and discouraging. Since 1964 we have seen participation criteria and requirements built into federal law. Office of Economic Opportunity programs, particularly Community Action Agencies, Rural Conservation and Development Programs of the Soil Conservation Service, the Regional Health Planning Councils, and even the private-voluntary Planned Parenthood program are illustrations of organizations that have a built-in requirement of clientele, user, or participant representation. It is true that the *reason* for building in these user components has varied. At one extreme is the belief that the social ailment of the moment is inherent in the individual and his family and that the person must be involved in affairs so that *he* can change. Others believe that the problem of poverty, for example (or any other social pathology), is in the institutions of the society and it is these that must be changed. According to this argument, only the participants or recipients are in a position to know the direction the change should take. (For further discussion, see [3, 9, 19, 24, 26, 32, 33, 36].)

As idealistic and as hopeful as plans have been for a participatory democracy, generally they have failed. Some commentators say that the middle class has been unwilling to share its control over resources and therefore won't permit participation. Others say that the poor and the disenfranchised have been unable or unwilling to change in order to match the values of a dominant society. Neither of these explanations gets us anywhere. Whole communities (or at least parts of communities) are being left on the margin. They have inadequate access to the services set as minimal—including health, education, housing, cultural recreation, and economic.

Participation has two edges. One is internal to the neighborhood and community, and it is internal relationships which add a sense of belonging to the lives of people. It is these which were the basis of the old "country life" ideology. When neighborhood and community systems are fragmented—lacking an identity, lacking the structural conditions which support recreational, economic, and social life—such systems only vaguely deserve classification as a unit. One can imagine developing the networks that can reconstruct these systems. Peter Goldmark's "new rural society" [17] hopes to do just that, but the problems are immense.

The second edge of participation is essentially external, i.e., in the relationship between the community and the world around it. The voice of the declining community is, one would suspect, unclear;

spoken softly if at all. One gets the impression that local government officials have a number of liabilities. They cannot represent their constituencies as their "fathers" did because their constituencies lack the homogeneity that would be necessary for them to do so. These local officials may not be the persons with the most influence in public affairs and therefore they face difficulties in implementing decisions. If their ties via education, occupation, and employment, and other potential relationships are weak or nonexistent, the information (or knowledge) they would need to process even routine decisions might be lacking. And finally, if they are inclined to act in a paternalistic fashion vis-a-vis their constituents—illustrated by the statement, "Mr. Sedgewick, if you have a problem with your culvert, just call me up and I'll send a man right out," rather than establishing a policy which would cover all culverts on Mr. Sedgewick's road—the possibility of developing long-range policies that will affect the development process are slight.

But the problems extend far beyond the character of local officials. In a structural sense they are faced with formidable odds. Organizations of all types are centralized, often in a county seat or in a metropolitan area. Here, not over there, is where the information is needed to give local officials viable alternatives. A recent study in Minnesota outlined the complicated process of encouraging industrial expansion and new growth. Needed information, even in its raw form is not easily accessible to the community already set in a process of decline. The complications and chaos are also indicated in a study of satellite communities in North Dakota by Nelson, et al. [30].

A multi-group, competing but dynamic system is, however, possible. A Florida study [25] which compared two counties found the one which was experiencing growth to be the one with many competing organizations and groups. Its multigroup structure showed elements of competition and of cooperation. It was open to new leaders and new ideas whereas the declining area was effectively closed in its entire leadership-political system [see 21, 39].

This chapter, eclectic in its charge and scope, has developed the thesis that the form and content of human relationships have changed in rural society. While the communities have changed, while residents in rural areas have become more and more dependent on numerous contacts beyond the boundaries of their neighborhoods, some structures such as local government remain. But a government official who must "produce" on the basis of knowledge of resources beyond the boundaries of his home cannot be selected for his post on honorific, or on the normative criteria that he somehow "fits" the community. And neither is he likely to fit the community in any case because the fabric—whatever it was—that made it a community, no longer exists.

What seems to be needed is the insertion of new information, new alternatives from which to choose. There are numerous illustrations in the community development literature of the innovation that is possible when local people join in projects of mutual support. I'm also impressed by the need to affect the structures that impose limitations on the people who live within them. Human well-being in its total sense should be part of our consideration and not just a person's access to employment. We need to know what kind of community is desired and then to find out what it will require to achieve that.

As easy as it is to say that the problem of the declining community is that of participation—both within it and with its surroundings —experiences in recent years have shown how difficult it is to achieve even a modicum of the goal of participatory democracy.

REFERENCES

1. Anderson, A. H. 1952. *Changes in farm population and rural life in four North Dakota counties.* Fargo: North Dakota Agricultural Experiment Station Bulletin 375.
2. Bell, Wendell, Hill, Richard J., and Wright, Charles R. 1961. *Public leadership.* San Francisco: Chandler Publishing Co.
3. Benson, J. Kenneth. 1971. Militant ideologies and organizational contexts: The war on poverty and the ideology of "black power." *Soc. Quart.* 12:328–39.
4. Bishop, Morris. 1962. *History of Cornell.* Ithaca: Cornell Univ. Press.
5. Chittick, Douglass. 1955. Growth and decline of South Dakota trade centers, 1901–1951. Brookings: South Dakota Agricultural Experiment Station Bulletin 448.
6. Conrad, Earl. 1956. *The trial of William Freeman.* New York: Lancer Books.
7. Crain, Robert L., and Rosenthal, Donald E. 1967. Community status as a dimension of local decision-making. *Am. Soc. Rev.* 32:970–84.
8. Cross, Whitney R. 1940. *The burned over district: The social and intellectual history of enthusiastic religion in western New York, 1800–1850.* New York: Harper Torchbooks.
9. Dubey, Sumati N. 1970. Community action programs and citizen participation: Issues and confusions. *Soc. Work* 15:76–84.
10. Eberts, Paul R. 1972. Consequences of changing social organization in the northeast. In *Papers of the workshop of current rural development regional research in the northeast.* Ithaca: Northeast Regional Center for Rural Development.
11. Eberts, Paul R., and Kluess, Pluma W. 1972. Major regional dimensions in the northeastern United States (mimeograph).
12. Fitchen, Janet M. 1973. Poverty: A view from the hills. Ph.D. thesis, Cornell University.

13. Freeman, Linton C., et al. 1960. Local community leadership. Syracuse University: Paper No. 15, University College.
14. Gee, Wilson. 1933. A qualitative study of rural population in a single township: 1900–1930. *Am. J. Soc.* 39:221.
15. Gillette, John M. 1911. The drift to the city in relation to the rural problem. *Am. J. Soc.* 16:656.
16. ———. 1929. Rural life. *Am. J. Soc.* 34:1,089–98.
17. Goldmark, Peter C. 1972. *The new rural society.* Yale University Seminars in Modern Journalism.
18. Harden, Warren R. 1960. Social and economic effects of community size. *Rural Soc.* 25:205.
19. Hillman, Arthur, and Seever, Frank. 1970. Elements of neighborhood organization. In Fred M. Cox, et al., eds. *Strategies of community organization.* Itasca, Ill.: F. E. Peacock Publishers.
20. Hoffer, C. R. 1935. Changes in retail and service facilities of rural trade centers in Michigan, 1900 and 1930. East Lansing: Michigan Agricultural Experiment Station Special Bulletin 261.
21. Hoggan, Daniel H. n.d. *State and local capability to share financial responsibility of water development with federal government.* Washington, D.C.: U.S. Water Resources Council.
22. Hooker, Elizabeth R. 1928. Leaders in village communities. *Soc. Forces* 6:605–14.
23. Jenkins, David R. 1940. *Growth and decline of agricultural villages.* New York: Teachers College.
24. Kanter, Rosabeth M. 1971. Some social issues in the community development corporation proposal. In Bennello, George and Dimitrios Roussopoulos, eds. *The case for participatory democracy.* New York: Grossman Publishers.
25. Kimbrough, Ralph B. 1964. *Informal county leadership structure and controls affecting educational policy decision-making.* Gainesville, Fla.: Cooperative Research Project No. 1324.
26. Kravitz, Sanford, and Kolodner, Ferne. 1969. Community action: Where has it been? Where will it go? *Ann. Am. Acad. Polit. Soc. Sci.* 385:30–40.
27. Landis, Paul H. 1933. The growth and decline of South Dakota trade centers, 1901–1923. Brookings: South Dakota Agricultural Experiment Station Bulletin 279.
28. Mather, William G. 1941. Income and social participation. *Am. Soc. Rev.* 6:380–83.
29. McKenzie, R. D. 1933. *The metropolitan community.* New York: McGraw-Hill.
30. Nelson, William C., et al. 1973. Satellite communities in North Dakota: The present situation and strategies for growth. Fargo: Agricultural Economic Miscellaneous Report No. 11.
31. O'Shea, Robert, and Gray, Shirlene B. 1966. Income and community participation. *Welfare Rev.* 4:10–13.
32. Perry, Stewart E. 1971. A note on the genesis of the community development corporation. In Bennello C. George and Dimitrios Roussopoulos, eds. *The case for participatory democracy.* New York: Grossman Publishers.
33. Piven, Frances. 1966. Participation of residents in neighborhood community action programs. *Soc. Work* 11:73–80.
34. Roche, John P. 1963. The curbing of the militant majority. *Reporter* 29:34–38.

35. ———. 1963. *The quest for the dream: The development of civil rights and human relations in modern America.* New York: Macmillan Co.
36. Rubin, Lillian. 1967. Maximum feasible participation: The origins, implications, and present status. *Poverty and Hum. Resour. Abstr.* 2(Nov.–Dec.): 12.
37. Schulze, Robert O. 1958. The role of economic dominants in community power structure. *Am. Soc. Rev.* 23:3–9.
38. Schulze, Robert O., and Blumberg, Leonard U. 1957. The determination of local power elites. *Am. J. Soc.* 63:290–96.
39. Sharkansky, Ira. 1968. *Spending in the American states.* Chicago: Rand McNally.
40. Swift, Bert. 1972. *Planning for local development: The case of Oneida-Herkimer counties.* Ithaca: New York State Colleges of Agriculture and Life Sciences and Human Ecology.
41. Walton, John. 1967. The vertical axis of community organization and the structure of power. *Southwest. Soc. Sci. Quart.* 48:353–68.

CHAPTER SEVEN

SERVICE STRUCTURE OF THE SMALL COMMUNITY: PROBLEMS AND OPTIONS FOR CHANGE

BERT L. ELLENBOGEN

A BASIC PRINCIPLE of social organization maintains that if a social unit (a formal organization, community, region, etc.) is to survive, much less grow and develop, it must fulfill the needs and aspirations of its members—at least relatively well. Moreover, in order to grow and develop, a social unit must take into account the goals and expectations of other social units and to some extent the broader society with which it transacts. In addition, social units in modernizing and modern societies are functionally interdependent on each other for maintenance and sustenance, although within this interdependency some units are more dependent than others.

This principle is applicable to small communities, which, for the purposes of this chapter, are defined as nonmetropolitan centers with less than 1,000 population.

What are some general structural characteristics that may be attributed to the small nonmetropolitan community?

STRUCTURAL FEATURES. If we use the framework of the trade center and trade area as applied to this type of community in the Upper Midwest, in a majority of instances it would fall within the category of a hamlet with an average of 6 to 7 retail functions. Other small nonmetropolitan communities would be classified [7] as "minimum convenience centers," averaging approximately 14 retail functions. Furthermore, when we consider the hierarchial arrangement by which innovations filter and spread in a system of growth centers, then these nonmetropolitan localities under 1,000 inhabit-

BERT L. ELLENBOGEN is Professor of Sociology, University of Minnesota.

ants are at the "end of the line." That is, many of these communities are late adopters of new programs and practices and some are probably "hard core nonadopters" [2].

Still another way to view the small community is in terms of the social stratification system. It does not seem unreasonable to hypothesize, from the limited data on hand, that nonmetropolitan localities under 1,000 population in the Upper Midwest rank low on the hierarchial arrangement by which scarce resources (e.g., education, income, prestige, power, etc.) are distributed [see 9, 12, 38]. In addition, much, if not most, of the social change that takes place within the small community is initiated and dominated by external organizations. Roland Warren [42] states: "Most of the basic uncontrolled changes which take place at the community level do so in relation to focus outside of the local community and are not subject to its deliberate control, as in the case of the general price levels, or changing production techniques. . . ." On the one hand, the structural features of the small nonmetropolitan community are characterized by high interdependence with the outside world and limited control over decisions affecting its future, while on the other hand traditional values of independence and self-sufficiency are said to persist [20, 40]. In a sense the small rural locality is pervaded by a social paradox which influences its perceptions of service needs as well as its ability to mobilize itself in order to ensure the availability of services [25].

Be that as it may, let us outline further the service structure of the small nonmetropolitan locality. These communities have had a history of serving local needs, although there are signs that those not within relative proximity to an urban center have experienced a reduction in retail functions over the last several decades [14, 18, 23, 24, 44].

SERVICES. The availability of institutional services throughout most small communities of the Upper Midwest seems to be going in the same general direction as that of other services. For example, schools continue to be consolidated and the number of school districts reduced. Equally significant has been the failure to expand the availability of library, counseling, and other auxiliary services in rural junior and senior high schools. In fact, recent cutbacks in federal and state funds have resulted in a reduction of the existing limited supportive services offered by rural schools [14, 33].

The overall decline in institutional services is also reflected in the rural church. Sometimes there has been an outright closing of a church; in other instances an interdenominational consolidation has taken place; while in still other rural areas the clergyman has been given a circuit consisting of churches in several communities [8, 21, 34].

Among the small communities of varying sizes there appear to be considerable differences in the service structure [28]. This is evident by the presence or absence of banking establishments. Obviously, banks are of great significance to farmers and small businessmen in carrying on their entrepreneurial activities. Banks facilitate financial transactions, ensure a secure place to keep savings and valuable possessions, and extend credit. Data from the State of Minnesota for 1972 [1] reveal that while 51 percent of localities with less than 1,000 inhabitants had a bank, these establishments were found in only 15 percent of the localities with less than 250 persons compared with 95 percent of communities with populations of 500 to 1,000.

One of the more pervasive concerns expressed by members of the small rural locality has been that of having a full-time resident physician. The decline of the local doctor in rural centers began more than 50 years ago and became accentuated following World War II. Evidence of this trend is found in Minnesota communities with fewer than 1,000 inhabitants. In 1912, approximately one-quarter of these communities had a resident doctor; by 1962 only 3 percent had a full-time physician [16]. There is also variation in the distribution of medical doctors among rural communities. A study conducted in four Upper Midwest states in 1965 [15] reported that about one-half of the rural towns with between 500 to 1,000 persons had a resident doctor, in contrast with only 5 percent for communities under 500. The researchers concluded that many of the communities reporting a physician at the time of the study could become no-physician towns in the future. Doctors in small localities were found to have a significantly higher median age than those in urban centers, and the authors expressed skepticism that these rural communities would be able to attract a replacement when the resident doctor died or retired. It is no surprise that medical specialists are an even greater rarity in the nonmetropolitan small locality [31].

Dentists likewise are not prominent, particularly in communities with under 500 population. Slightly over 18 percent of the small communities in Minnesota reported a resident dentist. Further study revealed that 52 percent of nonmetropolitan localities with 500–1,000 persons had a dentist, compared with 2 percent of the localities with fewer than 250 persons [4].

So far, we've sketched out components of the service structure of the small community without considering the quality of existing services. One would expect that services in localities with under 1,000 population generally would be inferior to those of larger population centers. If, for no other reasons, differences in prestige, financial rewards, and cultural opportunities offered by the small locality in contrast to the larger center are likely to attract personnel with less than the desired level of technical training and with a more restricted professional orientation. This disadvantage may be reflected in the quality of medical care, education, repair and maintenance of household appliances, and other services [19, 20, 35, 37]. But differences in quality may also apply to local government and the public officialdom of the small nonmetropolitan community. One finds, for example, the monetary reward for public officials in Minnesota, even on a part-time basis, not particularly attractive. The Minnesota Village Legal Code [26] sets a minimum stipend of $15 a month for the office of mayor and $10 a month for each councilman. In fact, the minimal stipend turns out to be the modal salary for these officials in communities under 500; in localities of 500 to 1,000 population, the modal remuneration is only somewhat higher—$23 a month for mayor and $18 a month for councilman.

One inference that might be drawn from the preceding analysis is that nonmetropolitan localities with under 1,000 inhabitants in the Upper Midwest tend to have limited differentiation and specialization of services. Likewise, within different size categories of the small community, variation exists as to the level of differentiation and specialization of the service structure. The incomplete nature of the data at hand does not permit the relationship between community size and differentiation of services to be tested. However, studies undertaken in other sections of the nation [13] have found these two variables to be significantly related but with size explaining somewhat less than half the variance. Several other variables (e.g., fluidity, horizontal linkage, mobilization, etc.) in addition to population size have been suggested [11, 13, 41] as explaining the level of differentiation of services. The extent of differentiation that can be expected in communities of different size, particularly those with less than 1,000 inhabitants is also open to question. It is contended, for example, that the social organization of the small locality is such that it seldom can attract and maintain a manufacturing establishment. Generally, this appears to be the case; yet some nonmetropolitan rural localities do have an industrial plant. About 25 percent of nonmetropolitan localities in Minnesota with 500 to 1,000 population were reported [30] to have some form of nonagricultural manufacturing establishment in 1971. Five percent of these localities had one plant employing between 100 and 500 employees.

The obvious question is under what social and economic conditions can the small locality and its immediate environs expect to have a manufacturing enterprise. Moreover, what are the social and economic costs and benefits of this type of productive enterprise to the locality and the surrounding area? Without verified knowledge to the proceeding questions, industrial development for many small localities may be merely an exercise in frustration. But even if a small community is able to attract an industrial plant, the disadvantages, in some instances, may be considerable [36].

Meanwhile, a wide range of efforts has been underway to expand the availability of services to the small community. A number of these programs have involved the collaborative efforts of federal and state agencies with local officials. Small rural communities without available library facilities are visited regularly by mobile units. Helicopter services link semiisolated localities without medical services to health care centers for the handling of acute emergency cases. Also, in some instances, local needs are being met by services available outside of, but accessible to, the small rural locality. For example, the Minn.-Dak. Health Planning Council is developing health resources and facilities in 16 counties in Minnesota and North Dakota [39].

One finds that some communities in the Upper Midwest have gained access to health services through multicounty planning councils. In other localities services have been introduced through regional organizations. For example, information and referral centers dealing with social services have been created; councils have been established to reduce poverty; a credit system has been developed for prospective businessmen wishing to enter the tourist industry, etc.

Still other types of organizational forms have been devised to modify the rural service structure. Some small localities have organized self-help programs to obtain a resident doctor or dentist or establish some facility defined as needed but lacking (e.g., recreational center, library, etc.). The Special District is another organizational form which has gained prominence as a political unit to facilitate local services. This political unit has been established to an increasing extent in the Upper Midwest over the last several decades in order to increase such services as fire protection and flood control [5, 6].

The ad hoc organizational forms established in reaction to the diverse interests and demands of the small community have created a different set of problems. In some instances, different organizational forms (e.g., multicommunity, regional, etc.) may compete in providing the same service, or, because of the difficulties of coordination, some service needs may go unmet. In any case, the multiplicity of organizational forms operating at different ecological levels and sometimes within both public and private sectors may seriously limit the attainment of service objectives.

PLANNING. Many of these new organizations are established in reaction to demand rather than in anticipation of the rural community's needs. Roland Warren [42] has referred to this type of planning as adaptive rather than ". . . any fundamental type which would change or redirect the major flow of events." To a considerable extent, therefore, the small community becomes the "target" of an almost incessant state of crisis. Crisis decision making may not be an anathema to planning, but it is apt to create a restricted time frame for formulating and implementing policy. In fact, within this context the definition of the problem itself tends to be restricted. But other restraints are also imposed. For example, the range of alternatives sought for mitigating the problem is circumscribed, the employment of technical expertise is underutilized, and the quality of the evaluation is limited. The latter restriction may be the most serious of all. Without an adequate evaluation, there is reduced probability of acquiring knowledge to curtail the error and increase the chance for success in future problem-solving experiences.

There are signs of more systematic efforts toward anticipating the future service needs of rural communities. Nevertheless, it is doubtful that most small communities can absorb the costs to possess locally all the services considered necessary. Under some circumstances it may be more feasible for the small locality to obtain access to certain services through a regional planning program. However, the implementation of regional planning is not without uncertainty, hazard, and difficulty. Nor, for that matter, is there professional concensus about the strategy and tactics of planning.

One of the most difficult aspects of the planning process is centered around the question of goal-setting [17, 32, 43]. If the unit for the planning program is regional, what input, if any, should the small community have for setting the goals of such a program? Moreover, if the small community is to contribute to the goal-setting of a regional planning program, who will represent the small community? Its officialdom? Its elite members? The rank and file of the community?

But no less controversial than goal-setting is the issue of whether or not the members of a target unit should be involved in the implementation of a planning program, particularly on a regional basis. Without exploring the pros and cons of this issue, note should be taken that the participation pattern of the contemporary small community does not demonstrate high involvement in local civic affairs. In fact, the small community has a low rate of political participation when compared with larger population centers [29, 40].

Hesitancy, if not indifference, by members of the small locality to participate in local government should not be too surprising. Actually, there are few, if any, organizational features in rural America or the society at large which are primarily committed to developing community participation in the government of local affairs. Warren Bloomberg [3] has stated:

> No institutional sector is devoted primarily to motivating participation in community affairs, developing needed skills among the citizenry and facilitating and organizing their involvement and participation in

the recognition, definition and resolution of community problems and issues. It is assumed that growing up in the United States almost automatically includes acquiring the motives and competences of citizenships and that members of the community in the normal course of events will become genuinely concerned from time to time about one or another community problem and will react vigorously. With the exception of elections and referendums, our ideology of local democracy would, therefore, seem to depend for its implementation more upon an informal and always emergent organization of community members than upon the formally organized institutional sectors.

Apparently, if increases in the availability of services to the small community are to take place within the context of regional planning, other structural changes will probably occur. One might expect a rise in external linkages and in the level of interdependence. But a decline might also occur in the small community's power position, which already has been defined as low. However, under certain conditions a coalition of communities may increase their collective control over corporate bodies (e.g., state and federal agencies) even though an individual community has sustained a loss of power [10]. There is a need for additional knowledge. We need to know the structural characteristics and the social consequences of coalition formation for a social unit such as the small community and whether this knowledge can be incorporated into the strategy and tactics of regional planning.

We should note that the plight of the small community has provided another example of our cultural preference in problem-solving for what has been termed [22]: "the neatness of exit over the heartbreak of voice." One consequence has been to almost mechanistically "write off" the small nonmetropolitan community like one or another problem segment of the society ("the poor," "the aged"). The fact is that significant efforts directed toward increasing the service structure of the small community, if carefully codified, could contribute valuable knowledge to aid in controlling the social environment of more complex ecological units within the society.

REFERENCES
1. *Bank Directory of the Upper Midwest.* 1972. Minneapolis: Commercial West.
2. Berry, Brian. 1972. Hierarchial diffusion: The basis of developmental filtering and spread in a system of growth centers. In Niles M. Hansen, ed. *Growth centers in regional economic development.* New York: Free Press.
3. Bloomberg, Warren. 1966. Community organization. In Howard S. Becker, ed. *Social problems: A modern approach.* New York: John Wiley and Sons.
4. Board of Dental Examiners. 1961. *Nineteen hundred and sixty roster of dentists and dental hygienists, registered in the state of Minnesota.* St. Paul.

5. Bolen, John C. 1957. *Special district government in the United States.* Berkeley: Univ. of California Press.
6. Boles, Donald. 1972. Adaption of local and regional government: The emerging special district. In *Proceedings of rural community development seminar: Focus on Iowa.* Ames: Center for Agricultural and Rural Development, Iowa State University. Section M.
7. Borchert, John, et al. 1963. *Trade centers and trade areas of the upper Midwest.* Upper Midwest Economic Study, Urban Report Number 3. Minneapolis: Univ. of Minnesota Press.
8. Burchard, Waldo. 1963. A comparison of urban and rural churches. *Rural Soc.* 28:271–78.
9. Clark, Terry, ed. 1968. *Community structure and decision-making: Comparative analyses.* Scranton: Chandler Publishing Co.
10. Coleman, James S. 1973. Loss of power. *Am. Soc. Rev.* 38:1–18.
11. Deutsch, Karl. 1961. Social mobilization and political development. *Am. Polit. Sci. Rev.* 55:483–514.
12. Duncan, Otis D., et al. 1956. *Social characteristics of urban and rural communities, 1950.* New York: John Wiley and Sons.
13. Eberts, Paul. 1972. Consequences of changing social organization in the northeast. In *Papers of the workshop of current rural development regional research in the northeast.* Ithaca: Northeast Regional Center for Rural Development, Cornell University.
14. Eldridge, Eber. 1972. Trends related to rural areas. In *Proceedings of rural community development seminar: Focus on Iowa.* Ames: Center for Agricultural and Rural Development, Iowa State University. Section B.
15. Fahs, Ivan, and Peterson, Osler. 1962. Towns without physicians and towns with only one—A study of four states in the upper Midwest, 1965. *Am. J. Public Health.* 58:1,200–11.
16. Fahs, Ivan, and Photiadis, John. 1962. Distribution of physicians in Minnesota, 1962. Department of Sociology, University of Minnesota (unpublished manuscript).
17. Friedemann, John. 1973. *Retracking America: A theory of transactive planning.* New York: Doubleday and Co.
18. Fuguitt, Glenn. 1963. The city and the countryside. *Rural Soc.* 28:246–61.
19. Gallaher, Art. 1961. *Plainville—Fifteen years later.* New York: Columbia Univ. Press.
20. Gross, Edward, and Donohue, George. 1970. Organizational diversity: The rural system as an ideal model. In *Benefits and burdens of rural development.* Ames: Iowa State Univ. Press.
21. Hassinger, Edward, and Holik, John. 1970. Changes in the number of rural churches in Missouri 1952–1967. *Rural Soc.* 35:354–67.
22. Hirschman, Albert. 1970. *Exit, voice and loyalty.* Cambridge: Harvard Univ. Press.
23. Hodge, Gerald. 1966. Do villages grow?—Some perspectives and predictions. *Rural Soc.* 31:183–96.
24. Johnson, H. E., and Fuguitt, Glenn. 1973. Changing retail activity in Wisconsin villages: 1939–1954–1970. *Rural Soc.* 38:207–18.
25. Larson, Olaf. 1961. Basic goals and values of farm people. In *Goals and values in agricultural policy.* Ames: Iowa State Univ. Press.
26. League of Minnesota Municipalities. 1973. *1973 salary survey municipalities under 2500.* Minneapolis: Municipal Reference Bureau, University of Minnesota.

27. MacQueen, John. 1972. A plan for the distribution of physicians and the health care units needed to provide health service in Iowa. In *Proceedings of rural community development seminar: Focus on Iowa.* Ames: Center for Agricultural and Rural Development, Iowa State University. Section L.

28. Mayer, Leo V. 1972. Delineation of Iowa communities with major economic attachment to agriculture. In *Proceedings of rural community development seminar: Focus on Iowa.* Ames: Center for Agricultural and Rural Development, Iowa State University. Section E.

29. Milbrath, Lester. 1965. *Political participation: How and why do people get involved in politics.* Chicago: Rand-McNally.

30. Research Division, Minnesota Department of Economic Development. 1972. *Minnesota directory of manufacturers, 1970–71.* St. Paul.

31. Peterson, Osler, and Fahs, Ivan. 1966. *Health manpower for the upper Midwest.* St. Paul: Hill Foundation.

32. Robinson, Ira, ed. 1971. *Decision-making in urban planning.* Beverly Hills, Calif.: Sage Publications.

33. Rogers, Everett, and Burdge, Rabel. 1972. *Social change in rural societies.* New York: Appleton-Century-Crofts.

34. Salesbury, W. Seward. 1964. *Religion in American culture.* Homewood, Ill.: Dorsey Press.

35. Sanders, Irwin. 1966. *The community,* 2nd ed. New York: Ronald Press.

36. Scott, John T., Jr., and Summers, Gene F. 1974. Problems in communities after industry arrives. In *Rural industrialization: Problems and potentials.* Ames: Iowa State Univ. Press.

37. Smith, T. L., and Zopf, Paul. 1970. *Principles of inductive rural sociology.* Philadelphia: F. A. Davis Co.

38. Sower, Christopher, et al. 1964. The changing power structure in agriculture: An analysis of negative versus positive organization power. In James Copp, ed. *Our changing rural society.* Ames: Iowa State Univ. Press.

39. Spilde, R., and Schmidt, B. 1971. West Minnesota profile. Moorhead: Moorhead State College.

40. Talbot, Ross, and Youngberg, I. Garth. 1972. The importance of political ideology in rural development. In *Proceedings of rural community development seminar: Focus on Iowa.* Ames: Center for Agricultural and Rural Development, Iowa State University. Section D.

41. Warren, Roland. 1963. *The community in America.* Chicago: Rand-McNally.

42. ———. 1968. The theory and strategy of community development. *Am. J. Agr. Econ.* 50:1,226–38.

43. ———. 1970. Toward a non-utopial normative model of the community. *Am. Soc. Rev.* 35:219–27.

44. Yoesting, Dean R., and Marshall, D. M. 1969. Trade pattern changes of open country residents: A longitudinal study. *Rural Soc.* 34:85–91.

CHAPTER EIGHT

ENHANCING ECONOMIC OPPORTUNITY

LUTHER TWEETEN

COMMUNITIES and the nation as a whole cannot be expected to stand aside and do nothing to enhance economic opportunities in rural areas. Two major approaches for enhancing economic opportunities in rural areas are: (1) local action to provide community services more efficiently and to create new jobs through industry, and (2) national efforts to promote equity and efficiency through programs to improve the structure of markets and meet the needs of persons unable to earn an adequate income.

The vast literature dealing with rural development is rewarding but highly fragmented. Anyone who would construct a comprehensive policy for development faced with such riches of disparity in the literature faces a major dilemma. Well aware of this, I wish to set forth a comprehensive program for enhancing economic opportunity in communities and areas characterized by either population decline or stability. Several important issues are dealt with: (1) increasing the quantity of local resources versus using existing resources more efficiently, (2) resolving local problems by action of the community itself versus action at the multicounty or national level, (3) the perennial dilemma of equity versus efficiency in development programs, and (4) whether to emphasize place or people prosperity in development programs.

LOCAL DECISIONS TO ENHANCE ECONOMIC BASE. Enhancing economic opportunity while experiencing population decline appears contradictory because net out-migration itself provides

LUTHER TWEETEN is Regents Professor, Department of Agricultural Economics, Oklahoma State University, Stillwater.

strong evidence of inadequate local employment. Some communities accept net out-migration to relieve stress on the local resource base and decrease the man-land ratio. By so doing, they increase returns per unit of remaining labor resources and enhance the tax base per capita. The earnings per farm worker and tax base per person would surely be substantially lower today in the absence of net out-migration from farming. National income also would be much lower. Growing awareness of environmental and other problems stemming from population growth and the desire to retain the attractive natural environment of rural communities has dampened the spirit of growth.

However, many communities desire to maintain their population to avoid redundant infrastructure, to use their available services efficiently, and as a matter of pride. Much new economic activity does not have undesirable environmental effects and adds substantially to incomes and living standards of local residents. The process of adjusting to a new environment can be traumatic for movers. Many persons place great value on staying in their home community to be near friends, parents, and familiar surroundings; local job growth reduces the personal cost of exercising that option.

The economic base of many rural communities is farming. Since farm management specialists continually are appraising opportunities to raise farm incomes, I shall not dwell on this issue. Many communities see limited opportunities for maintaining their population because of increased farm technology and slow growth in demand for farm products, and so they wish to explore other sources of an economic base such as manufacturing. There is evidence that nonmetropolitan communities are increasingly attractive to industry. The manufacturing wage and salary employment increased 12 percent in metropolitan areas and 31 percent in nonmetro areas between 1960 and 1970 [6]. Furthermore, the gains in employment and population were rather widely dispersed among all but the very smallest communities. Although the specter of 15,000 local development corporations chasing something on the order of 1,000 new firms each year invites skepticism, communities in large numbers will continue to enhance their economic base through new industry.

The location of new industry and the expansion of existing firms is influenced by three principle factors: availability of inputs, markets, and transportation.

Markets. Closeness to markets is frequently decisive in industry location. Nationally, nearly three-fourths of new jobs are in service industries such as finance, trade, and government. Primary service industry requires an educated labor force, few natural resources, and wishes to be near large centers of population to directly serve their customers. Secondary service industry exists to serve basic industry and spontaneously develops after industries such as manufacturing create jobs. Thus the strategy best suited to nonmetro communities is to first develop primary industry such as manufacturing, then expect to see secondary and even primary service industries develop as employment and income grow. An example is the Piedmont region of the Southeast, which is developing primary service industry to complement its economic base that earlier was weighted toward low wage occupations. In contrast to earlier decades, the region is now making impressive advances in income and population.

Inputs. Firms requiring large quantities of bulky raw materials locate near the source of these inputs. Industry is becoming less natural-resources-oriented and thus has lessening need to locate near soil, mineral, forest, and potential fishing resources. It increasingly seeks to be near consumers or suppliers of intermediate inputs. For example, automobile makers wish to be near firms which can supply tires and other components not manufactured by the auto company itself. Often the decisive input is labor. The quality of labor is often more important than the quantity. Even though substantial unskilled labor is available, a firm may not find it profitable to locate and utilize such labor unless adequate amounts of skilled labor are available as well. Attitudes of workers also are important. A community which is known for labor unrest, frequent strikes, and militant labor unions is likely to be bypassed by locating firms.

Transportation. Another major economic factor determining industry location is the availability of transportation. The community which is near an interstate highway, a railroad line, and a major airport has a distinct advantage. While transportation is a smaller part of costs than in earlier times, still a change in the transportation rate can determine the success or failure of efforts to attract a firm. For example, the reduction in rail rates for the shipment of wheat grain compared to flour encouraged flour mills to move from the Great Plains, near the source of their supply, to large population centers, their major markets.

Many industries can produce additional units of outputs at lower cost, other things equal, in large plants than in small plants—a large local pool of labor, intermediate inputs, adequate markets, and transportation combined with economies of plant size give rise to *economies of agglomeration*.

Secondary Factors. Many rural residents live either in or near communities which satisfy the three principal location factors for at least some industry. If these three factors are satisfied, then the final decision hinges on secondary factors including community characteristics, availability of building and site, concessions, and state and local tax rates. Whereas the community frequently can do little about the principal factors, it often can do much about the secondary factors.

To be realistic, rural communities must recognize that they are at a disadvantage competing with larger cities to supply adequate skilled labor, favorable markets, low cost transportation, and agglomeration economies. They are also frequently disadvantaged in secondary factors such as high quality services and housing. To obtain industry in the face of these deficiencies, it is necessary to provide concessions which can take the form of wages below what industry would have to pay in larger communities, exemptions from local property taxes, provision of building and site at low cost, or provision of utilities and credit at favorable rates. These concessions are likely to be minimized if efforts are concentrated on bringing industry to growth centers of 20,000 or more population within commuting distance of rural workers, or if the industry is originated by local entrepreneurs.

What Communities Spend to Attract Industry. Based on data from twelve new or expanded industrial plants located in five communities in the low income Ozarks region of eastern Oklahoma, the net gains to each community from new jobs were computed by Ronald Shaffer [26] in 1972. Activities of the firms ranged from steel fabrication and manufacturing of electronic components to vegetable canning and pecan shelling.

Net benefits to the community from each firm were divided into three components. The first component was private sector gains defined as plant payroll spent in the community less costs in the form of income foregone from jobs not refilled in the community when workers were employed at the new plant. Net benefits to the municipal sector, the second component, were computed as additional municipal utility receipts and taxes less the additional costs of utilities, other services, and financial concessions provided by the municipal government to the new firm. Net benefits to the school sector, the third component, were composed of additional taxes paid because of the new plant, plus additional state aid, less the costs of schooling the children of workers in the new plant. Costs and benefits pertained only to the community—outside economic activity was excluded.

Most of the industries were originated by local persons, but others were attracted by means including municipal development bonds, concessional Economic Development Administration loans, low rent or low cost plant site building, market information (on labor, raw materials, and transportation), vocational-technical training of the labor force, transportation facilities (e.g., rail or road spur), and special rates on water, gas, electricity, and sewer utilities.

Annual net benefits for the entire community were positive for each plant and averaged $3,772 per employee for all plants. Gains for each of the various communities ranged from a low of $2,072 to a high of $5,203 per employee. In a number of cases, however, the municipal sector and the schooling sector were made worse off by the attraction of new industry. Either taxes were raised or the community lowered the quality of services (or at least spent less per recipient) to accommodate new industry in these cases.

The average net gain of $3,772 per employee may occur annually for several years. The maximum subsidy that a community can provide a firm and just break even depends on how long the firm will remain in the community. Based on the annual benefit indicated above, the total subsidy that could be provided per employee averaged $15,891 if the plant operated 5 years and $27,772 if for 10 years based on a discount rate of 6 percent. These figures not only indicate the capitalized breakeven subsidy, but also the potential cost to the community from premature failure of the plant. The community loss averages $27,889 per employee if the plant receives a lump sum subsidy based on an assumed life of 20 years and fails after only 5 years of operation.

Although they appear high, these maximum inducements to get an industry to locate in a community are reinforced by other studies. A Wisconsin study of 130 firms found a rate of return of 500 percent on industrial subsidies. Studies [26, and others] in Mississippi and Illinois indicated respective rates of return of 800 percent and 900 percent on industrial subsidies. A 1972 advertisement in *Forbes* magazine indicated that the Canadian government would provide a subsidy of $30,000 per worker for firms that would locate in selected areas of Canada.

In general, the attraction of new jobs tends to have the highest payoff to the community where considerable underemployment exists, such as in the depressed Ozarks region of eastern Oklahoma. Few workers were brought from outside areas. An analysis [31] in Indiana where underemployment is low indicates much smaller net benefits in a community per employee from new jobs.

The conclusion is that net benefits are substantial to communities successful in obtaining new industries. But I am not recommending that these maximum subsidies be offered to firms by rural communities. Consideration needs to be given to each community's goals as well as to the cost of potential pollution, unsuccessful negotiations, and risk of firm exodus or failure. Each community should pursue the best terms available if it decides to seek new sources of income. Communities would also do well to first examine their backyards; some of the most successful industry ventures are new or expanded activities "home grown" by local entrepreneurs.

While, on the average, community net gains from new firms are substantial, they are not evenly distributed in the community. The majority of benefits accrue to the private sector. The municipal sector and the schools are sometimes worse off. Communities which attract industry just to take the pressure off the local tax base are likely to be disappointed, and even most successful industrial plants cause grievances. Winnebago Industries at Forest City, Iowa, brings massive economic benefits to a rural community of 4,000 people; but many farmers and retired residents who receive no tangible benefits see their taxes rise to support schools for children of factory workers who move into low cost housing in the community and pay few local taxes.

USING COMMUNITY RESOURCES MORE EFFICIENTLY. Numerous government agencies as well as local leaders focus on raising community real income through more efficient use of resources. The federal-state extension service has helped to identify community leaders and community goals and to organize for action to reach community goals. State and multicounty planning specialists, the Economic Development Administration, and the Department of Housing and Urban Development "701" planning grants have assisted in formulating comprehensive development and land use plans to better utilize resources. Rural zoning—a measure which can prevent urban sprawl, prohibit nuisance enterprises from encroachment, preserve historic and scenic attractions, and protect farmland while providing for orderly development—is receiving wider support from rural people and raises long-run real income through better resource use.

Whether a community declines gracefully in population, holds steady, or grows, it is likely to want efficient delivery of community services. A growing body of literature [5, 10, 16, 17, 19] suggests ways to reduce the cost or raise the quantity (and quality) of services such as schooling, health care, and utilities in rural areas. In health care, approaches are being used such as volunteer ambulance services, prepaid monthly fees for comprehensive health care under group medical practice (health maintenance organizations), helicopter emergency ambulance service, use of paramedical professionals (e.g., former military medical corpsmen assisting medical dotcors), registered nurses in remote rural areas tied by space-age communications to medical doctors located at a major medical center, and provision of hospital-type services in nursing homes. In the case of schooling, savings can arise from use of paraprofessional assistants, multicounty district vocational schools, and electronic teaching aids.

Throughout the studies of services and local government administration, a finding that recurred was potential saving from consolidation of units to achieve economies of size. Yet the Census of Governments reported 78,268 governmental units in 1972, a decline of only 3,031 since 1967. The decline was almost entirely attributed to the reduction in the number of school districts from 21,782 in 1967 (34,678 in 1962) to 15,780 in 1972, reflecting legislative pressures as well as economic advantages from consolidation.

Another method of saving on community resources is to encourage farmers to build their new houses in town rather than in the open country and to commute to the farms [2]. The opportunity should be strictly voluntary, but it could be compensated from money saved by not having to furnish postal, school bus, and in some instances first class roads to farmsteads.

Increasing the efficiency of local resource use is a laudable and continuing need. But my belief is that efficient use of local resources alone cannot provide adequate community services and levels of living for declining rural communities. Outside assistance is essential and justified. Problems and opportunities spill over community, county, and state boundaries in a complex, interrelated political economy characterized by high migration rates, environmental pollution, and other problems. My belief is that local government should deal with local problems where possible, but that many local problems require multicounty district, state, or national government participation to be resolved.

NATIONWIDE PROGRAMS ENHANCING ECONOMIC OPPORTUNITY BASED ON PRINCIPLES OF EQUITY. In

general, programs that rank high in efficiency measured by cost-benefit ratios or rates of return on investment rank low in equity, defined as providing the most benefits to those with fewest resources [30]. One of the lessons learned from the "war on poverty" of the 1960s is that it is prohibitively expensive to compensate through remedial education programs (such as Head Start and the Job Corps) for poor family environment, ill health, and discrimination that stifled the development of competence. A related lesson is that the schooling has only a minor impact on economic outcomes compared to fate and the home. The nationwide "equal educational opportunity survey" [14] was originated to document the lack of schooling resources devoted to the disadvantaged. This survey rested on the proposition that provision of equal educational opportunity would mean lifting the socioeconomic position of the disadvantaged. The findings from the survey eventually led to a very nearly opposite conclusion: Providing equal educational resources or even outcomes measured by achievement scores would have nominal impact on narrowing the income disparities in the nation. Rates of return on investment in schooling

have been found to be favorable [9], and I believe that providing equal educational opportunity is imperative. *But more direct efforts are needed to deal with problems of low income.* Proposals for reform of welfare, school funding, and taxes discussed below treat this equity issue.

School Funding Reform. It is a well-documented fact that out-migration selects toward the young and well educated, depleting an area of human resources it can ill afford to lose if it is to attract outside private investment and have progressive local leadership.

Out-migration exits vast amounts of local capital. The private cost of raising a rural child (low-cost food plan) to age 18 in the North Central region was over $19,000 in 1969 expressed in dollars of that year [23]. With net out-migration of 40 million persons from farming alone since 1929, the human capital outflow approaches $1 trillion. The public cost of schooling, counting only the local portion financed with property taxes, averaged approximately $6,000 per migrant. Earnings from that investment accrue elsewhere when the high school graduate leaves.

Retaining all its young people is not a realistic alternative for any nonmetro community. Economically distressed rural communities in eastern Oklahoma lost up to 96 percent of their young people through migration, medium-sized communities lost 85 percent, and even the fast-growing prosperous large urban centers lost 72 percent of their young people through out-migration [11].

Two approaches to avoid severe capital depletion exist. One is for the community to attract immigrants who offset the outflow of community capital and who generate earnings to maintain community services. The second alternative is to receive compensation for net outflow of local investment in the schooling. While school funding procedures [9] have been devised to compensate for loss of schooling capital through net out-migration, a less complicated approach would be simply for each state and the federal government to assume a large share of the cost of common schools. Compensation for net outflow of capital can be justified on efficiency as well as equity grounds, because communities which experience high net out-migration underinvest in schooling relative to their ability as measured by the percent of local income spent on schooling [33].

Tax Reform. Studies in Iowa, Oklahoma, and other states [13] show that the farmer pays considerably higher total taxes in relation to his income than the nonfarmer, primarily because of property taxes. Less reliance on property taxes would raise the disposable income of farmers, but reforms to raise capital gains tax rates to the level of rates on earnings could offset this gain. Tax loopholes such as exemptions for interest on state and municipal bonds benefit the wealthy. This loophole could be removed and replaced by a federal government subsidy on state and municipal bonds with $2 gained by the federal government in tax revenues for each dollar it would cost the federal government to subsidize state and local bonds at the level of terms currently available. Extended treatment of tax reform issues is found elsewhere [21, 22].

Welfare Reform. Export base theory, a cornerstone of regional economics, stresses that a region grows by developing export industries, defined as activities that bring dollars from outside a community or region. Welfare reform, with federal takeover of public assistance programs, would bring in dollars and as such, public assistance may be defined as an "export industry." The argument for reform rests on grounds of efficiency as well as equity.

On efficiency grounds, a given real income to those receiving public assistance can be provided at lower costs in a rural area than in the metropolis. People move from depressed rural areas which provide low payments, to metropolitan areas where payments are far more generous. Ghetto problems of low incomes, high incidence of welfare, crime, and drug abuse frequently are associated with residents who one or two generations earlier were living in rural areas which seemed to accommodate such persons with fewer social problems than encountered in the ghetto. New York City obviously has a stake in welfare reform in Mississippi, for example.

The need for welfare reform rests in majority on issues of horizontal equity. States with the least ability to finance an adequate public assistance program also have the greatest need. This factor helps explain why the state of New York provided an average monthly payment of $288 per family on Aid to Families with Dependent Children (AFDC) in 1971 while the state of Mississippi provided only $55. Since rural states are frequently poor states, they stand to benefit most from federal takeover (already underway for public assistance categories other than AFDC) of all public assistance which would equalize payments among states [3]. The past neglect of the rural poor is implicit in the estimate that of the $3 billion net increase in outlays for public assistance under the Family Assistance Plan, half would go for rural people although rural people comprise one-fourth of the nation's population [8]. The working poor, especially prominent in rural areas, frequently have less income than welfare recipients. Major welfare reform proposals include the working poor.

Three major income maintenance proposals are (1) the demogrant plan, which would provide a continuing grant to every person scaled as deemed appropriate for age and place in the family [20]; (2) the negative income tax [24], which would provide a guaranteed $2,400, for example, to a family of four with 50 cents deducted from that guarantee for each dollar earned by the family up to a breakeven level of $4,800 of earnings; and (3) a wage (or earnings) supplement [see 7], which would provide a payment of 50 percent of the difference between a target wage of $2.50 per hour and the actual wage. Adoption of any one of these proposals would be a boon to rural people and would add substantially to the economic base of rural communities.

After these issues with primary regard for equity are treated, then other programs and policies should be administered with primary regard for efficiency. And since private enterprise has demonstrated ability to perform efficiently, it should be encouraged, constrained only by measures needed to make markets function more efficiently with private incentives corrected to reflect social priorities through a system of taxes and subsidies.

NATIONWIDE PROGRAMS ENHANCING ECONOMIC OPPORTUNITY BY IMPROVING MARKET STRUCTURE AND INCENTIVES. Public opinion polls record vast disenchantment with large cities. A nationwide Gallup Poll [see 25] in 1972 found that about half of all persons interviewed preferred their current place of residence, but the percentage dropped from 80 to 55 to 39 percent, respectively, from rural to small urban to large urban center residents. Whereas 90 percent of rural residents who were past rural residents preferred rural residence, only 46 percent of the large-urban residents who were past large-urban residents preferred their current place of residence. Only 27 percent of past rural residents residing in large urban centers at the time of the poll preferred to reside in that setting. Moreover, disenchantment with the city is growing. The proportion of respondents preferring city life fell from 22 percent in 1966 to 13 percent in 1972, while the proportion preferring rural residence increased from 49 percent to 55 percent.

The principal reasons stated by respondents for not carrying out their preferences were economic. It appears that the wishes of people are secondary—the location of people depends on the location of jobs (and public assistance) which in turn depends on the decisions made by firms and public officials.

Before we rush into premature policies to permit people to live in the place of their choice, let's examine further the empirical evidence. Four attitudes that relate to personal effectiveness and well-being were found to be for the most part unaffected by place of residence but were instead a function of education, income, and occupation. The implication is that place of residence, per se, need not be the focal point for centrifugal policies of balanced growth, population redistribution, and decentralization. Personal satisfactions will be improved only if opportunities for income, occupation, and education attend a change in place of residence. People will only be made worse off if public policy sends them to rural areas that are unable to provide adequate economic opportunity.

At least two important economic dimensions exist in the location of economic activity so that the limited resources of this nation can provide the greatest real output. One concerns the provision of public goods and services; the other private goods and services.

The costs of providing a given quality of a large number of public services have been estimated for cities of various sizes by Douglas Morris [17]. After accounting for externalities, the least cost per capita is in cities of 20,000–1,000,000 residents. Costs in smaller cities and open country are high because of the large per capita cost for schools, health care, utilities, and fire protection. Costs in larger cities are high because of the large per capita cost for crime prevention, pollution control, and traffic congestion control.

Another study [12] examines efficient location of private firms by estimating profit rates by industry by place of residence. Preliminary results indicate that profit rates within a given industry do not differ significantly by city size. While one interpretation of these findings is that industry can locate anywhere and is equally efficient whatever its location, a more realistic inference is that industry does respond rather quickly to comparative profit incentives and locates where it can make the greatest profit. The latter conclusion also follows if firms locate at random and those which do not make profits fail. In any event, overall industry performance appears to be satisfactory—firms locate in a manner to maximize private economic efficiency.

But the economic efficiency thereof is myopic, equating private marginal costs and returns. If private costs (benefits) differ from social costs (benefits), then superb industry performance measured by adherence to principles of profit maximization and equating of costs and returns at the margin does not maximize social real income. Evidence points to the need to change the structure and incentives rather than the performance of the market to raise social efficiency.

Numerous distortions in the market, which impede adjustments society finds optimal, at the same time operate to the disadvantage of rural areas. One element is labor costs. Underemployment frequently exceeds 30 percent in rural counties because rural living is a way of life and people are reluctant to go to large urban centers for jobs even if jobs are available [15]. In other instances, workers have returned home to rural areas after an unsuccessful stay in the city where they could not get or hold a job because of low skills and lack of experience.

Underemployed rural labor has low opportunity cost because

tle output is foregone as workers are employed in new local industry. Farm output frequently expands as operators are employed elsewhere and units are consolidated. Minimum wage laws, high costs of paperwork for social programs such as social security and unemployment insurance, and labor unions coupled with concepts of a socially acceptable wage all combine to create inflexible wage rates and to make employers pay actual wages above rates that would utilize underemployed rural labor at a profit. If Ford or General Motors must pay a union wage, then they can most profitably locate their plants in large cities where there are more skilled workers.

Another imperfection in the market is externalities. Firms in large urban centers do not pay the full costs for control of crime, air pollution, and transportation congestion which attends the agglomeration of jobs and people in densely populated areas. If firms in rural areas (or in growth centers of 20,000–1,000,000 residents within commuting distance of rural workers) were allowed to pay the low-opportunity cost of labor and if firms in metropolitan areas were taxed for the full social costs of these externalities, decentralization would be speeded. Some costs of congestion are charged to the firm because workers demand higher wages to compensate for traffic congestion (although workers are constrained in their demands if jobs are unavailable elsewhere). Other costs of congestion do not accrue to firms because workers are unwilling to accept the fact that their lives will be cut short by air pollution.

A system of taxes and subsidies can align social costs (benefits) with private costs (benefits) and create incentives for firms to locate where social efficiency is greatest. Because the taxes on private firms which are to adjust for urban externalities are politically unacceptable, a system of positive incentives to firms that locate in nonmetro areas is more appealing. These incentives could take a number of forms. I suggest that locating firms could take write-offs from federal income axes that could be tied to the degree of underemployment in an area.
ˋ alternative or complementary program is to terminate minimum
ˋ laws and replace them with a wage supplement program to ac-
ˋish the intent of minimum wages (provide an acceptable wage
ˋkilled workers) but which in fact do the opposite (they cause
ˋ be unemployed).
ˋal of improving the efficiency of markets calls for a feder-
ˋrogram of worker-relocation financial assistance, counsel-
ˋng in areas that are unable or unwilling to create jobs
ˋts. Such programs have been found to have favorable
ˋnd can direct workers to places where jobs are more
ˋ adequate community services can be provided at
One major role of economic planning would be
ˋmal mix of industry location incentives and

worker mobility incentives to a given region or multicounty district. People in areas unable or unwilling to provide jobs would be eligible for financial assistance to help workers relocate where jobs are available; areas willing and able to attract jobs with location incentives set at the level necessary to overcome market imperfections would be provided inducements for industry location and job creation.

SUMMARY AND CONCLUSIONS. To enhance economic opportunity in rural areas in the face of declining employment in farming and mining requires perceptive local leadership, planning, and action. A community can enhance economic opportunity through local action to broaden the resource base through industry or other means, or to use the existing resource base more efficiently. While local measures are worthy and deserving of full support in their own right, they should not obscure the fact that the majority of rural communities declining in population cannot provide adequate services (including education for migrants who leave) and avoid anomie without outside help [1].

I view programs to enhance economic opportunity in rural areas as an integral part of a nationwide policy to foster a more equitable and efficient economic system. It rests on the judgment that public policy should first deal with problems of equity through tax, welfare, and school funding reform; then deal with problems of efficiency by changing the structure and incentives facing industry.

Equity entails providing low income persons with means to avoid deprivation, treating those in similar economic circumstances alike, and compensating for economic spillover. A comprehensive income maintenance program could provide the working poor with incomes at least as high as those on welfare, encourage family stability, maintain work incentives, align payment rates among the states, and shift costs to the federal government in recognition of the inability of some states to provide assistance at levels that keep social problems from spilling over into other states. School funding reform could at once provide outlays for an adequate curriculum, align local taxes with ability to pay, and compensate schools for net spillout of benefits.

Economists are upset by the preoccupation of communities with attracting new jobs rather than with preparing their youth for employment elsewhere. A closer look confirms the economic rationality of the community: Its choice is generating a new job *adding* $3,772 per worker versus exodus of a high school graduate *subtracting* $6,000 of local capital. School funding reform could align community incentives with society's incentives. Tax reform could adjust for high property taxes paid by farmers in relation to income. Intervention is warranted in other instances where activity in one political jurisdiction spills over into other areas. Examples include assistance for pollution control that benefits "downstream" parties and zoning to prevent urban sprawl and promote orderly development.

With the above programs to promote equity and compensate for spillovers, the remaining national policy for rural development should focus on efficiency—improving the market structure and incentives of private industry in making location decisions with maximum free choice left to firms. Incentives to private firms would align social costs (benefits) with private costs (benefits). Means include a system of tax write-offs to industry geared to underemployment in an area, a wage supplement to reduce the private cost of underemployed rural labor to the real cost, and labor mobility assistance to overcome lack of knowledge, capital constraints, and other impediments to efficient functioning of labor markets.

Several notable corollaries follow from the suggested basic policy. People should be free to locate where they want subject to their paying the social costs as well as receiving benefits of that location. Accordingly, all federal programs that subsidize community services and encourage people to locate in socially inefficient places should be terminated. Federal grants to local governments for urban renewal, mass transit, and model cities, as well as revenue sharing funds obviously have little justification in this framework. Since the federal government can borrow or guarantee loans on better terms than others in many instances, concessional loans for water, sewer, electrical, and telephone systems and for other infrastructure can be justified.

Categorical grants to communities are inefficient means to help low income people; few dollars trickle down [32]. Target efficiency is much greater if welfare assistance is provided to *families* rather than *communities*. Grants to communities to improve utilities and other services for the purpose of making them more attractive to industry also have low target efficiency (many funds go to communities that are unsuccessful in getting new jobs) and should be terminated.

Most payment-in-kind welfare programs for housing and other services have low target efficiency, with a small proportion of the dollars spent on them going to the poor. And in-kind programs with high target efficiency such as food stamps and public housing could be replaced by an increase in cash income maintenance payments. The justification for payment-in-kind is that low income people spend unwisely and need to have their budgets set by outsiders. If competent spending is measured by high budget proportions devoted to necessities such as food, clothing, and shelter, then low income people are the most competent spenders of all. A given amount of real income can be provided to low income people at less cost to the public through cash assistance.

Emphasis on growth centers in development appears to be dead for now, the victim of misguided metropolitan enthusiasts who claimed cities of 20,000–250,000 were too small for economic viability and rural enthusiasts who claimed cities of that size were too remote, who saw no need to focus development efforts and who saw every community as an opportunity for job growth. The growth center concept should not be forgotten, however, even if it is not stressed in current legislation. Growth centers offer industry a large pool of labor and other inputs, adequate transportation, markets and agglomerative economies, and the cultural and other secondary location advantages mentioned earlier. Growth centers offer workers an alternative to the unfortunate "company town" with a single major employer (monopsony); give continuity to employment through having employment alternatives when one firm fails, moves, or exploits workers; and provide access to a wide array of quality services at reasonable cost.

An evaluation of policy for rural communities would be incomplete without a look at allocation of resources among various phases of rural development: organization-plans-action. The first two phases will be unproductive without strong financial support for action programs through national efforts outlined earlier to create jobs and reduce the cost of labor mobility. What organization, planning, and self-help can do for rural communities has consistently been overestimated, while national funding required to overcome job market imperfections has consistently been underestimated. If rural development programs have not worked, it is because they have never really been tried (i.e., programs provided few funds essential to follow organizing and planning). The Rural Development Act of 1972 appears to be no exception [28]. Rural development programs can be likened to construction of a building. The services of carpenters (development specialists) have been obtained, architects (development planners) have been busy, and these groups have produced some worthwhile results. However, real action awaits provision of "construction materials."

The development plan outlined here would eliminate many existing fragmented programs and bureaucracy. By targeting limited funds for equity in meeting needs of people with low incomes and for efficiency in encouraging private industry to create jobs where social net returns are greatest, the plan would do much to enhance economic opportunity in rural communities which have not been served fairly in past programs.

REFERENCES

1. Bills, Nelson, and Barkley, Paul. 1973. Public investment and population changes in three rural Washington state towns. Agricultural Economic Report No. 236. Economic Research Service in cooperation with Washington State Agricultural Experiment Station.

2. Bond, Larry, and Gardner, B. Delworth. 1971. A theoretical framework for analyzing residence shifts of farm families. *Intermountain Econ. Rev.* 2:47–59.
3. Dresch, Stephen. 1972. Assessing the differential regional consequences of federal tax-transfer policy. *Proceedings of Regional Economic Development Conference* (EDA OER-72-004). Washington, D.C.: U.S. Department of Commerce.
4. Gardner, B. Delworth. 1970. Toward a population distribution policy for the United States. Proceedings of 43rd Meeting of the Western Agricultural Economics Association, Tuscon, Arizona, July 1970.
5. Hall, J. Patrick, and Jones, Lonnie. 1973. Costs of solid waste management in rural communities in Texas. *South. J. Agr. Econ.* 5:115–19.
6. Haren, Claude C. 1972. Table of employment by industry from 1960–1970. In *Rural development chartbook* (ERS-500). Washington, D.C.: U.S. Department of Agriculture.
7. Haveman, Robert A. 1972. Work conditioned subsidies as an income maintenance strategy: Issues of program structure and integration. Institute for Research on Poverty Discussion Paper 141-72. Madison: University of Wisconsin.
8. Hines, Fred, and Jordan, Max. 1971. *Welfare reform: Benefits and incentives in rural areas* (ERS-470). Washington, D.C.: U.S. Department of Agriculture.
9. Hines, Fred, and Tweeten, Luther. 1972. Optimal regional funding of elementary and secondary schooling. Research Report P-669. Stillwater: Oklahoma Agricultural Experiment Station.
10. Hitzhusen, Frederick. 1973. Some measurement criteria for community service output and costs: The case of fire protection in Texas. *South. J. Agr. Econ.* 5:99–107.
11. Holland, David. 1972. The geographic and income class distribution of the benefits of public education. Unpublished Ph.D. thesis. Stillwater: Department of Agricultural Economics, Oklahoma State University.
12. Janssen, Larry. 1974. Comparative profit rates of U.S. manufacturing firms by city size. Unpublished M.S. thesis. Stillwater: Department of Agricultural Economics, Oklahoma State University.
13. Janssen, Larry, and Tweeten, Luther. 1973. The property tax in Oklahoma. *Okla. Bus. Bull.* Norman: University of Oklahoma.
14. Jencks, Christopher, et al. 1972. *Inequality.* New York: Basic Books.
15. Kampe, Ronald, and William Lindamood. 1969. Underemployment estimates by county, 1960. Agricultural Economic Report No. 116. Washington, D.C.: U.S. Department of Agriculture.
16. Leadley, S. M., ed. 1971. *Working papers on rural community services.* Proceedings of National Workshop on Problems of Research on Delivery of Community Services in Rural Areas, 13–16 December 1971, Nebraska Center for Continuing Education at Lincoln.
17. Morris, Douglas. 1973. Economies of city size. Unpublished Ph.D. thesis. Stillwater: Department of Agricultural Economics, Oklahoma State University.
18. Nelson, James, and Tweeten, Luther. 1973. Subsidized labor mobility—An alternative use of development funds. Journal Article 2481 of the Agricultural Experiment Station (mimeo.). Stillwater: Oklahoma State University.
19. Oklahoma Agricultural Experiment Station. 1972. Research application in rural economic development and planning. Research Report P-665. Stillwater: Oklahoma State University.

20. Okner, Benjamin. 1972. The role of demogrants as an income mainte-
    nance alternative (mimeo, prepared for IRP-JEC Conference on the
    Integration of Income Maintenance Programs). Madison: University of
    Wisconsin.
21. Pechman, Joseph. 1971. *Federal tax policy.* Washington, D.C.: Brook-
    ings Institution.
22. Pechman, Joseph, and Okner, Benjamin. 1972. Alternative sources of
    federal revenue. In Charles Schultz, et al., eds. *Setting national prior-
    ities: The 1973 budget.* Washington, D.C.: Brookings Institution.
23. Pennock, Jean L. 1970. Cost of raising a child. *47th Annual Agricul-
    tural Outlook Conference.* Washington, D.C.: U.S. Department of
    Agriculture.
24. President's Commission on Income Maintenance Programs (PCIMP).
    1969. *Poverty amid plenty.* Washington, D.C.: U.S. Government Print-
    ing Office.
25. Public Opinion. 1973. *Area development interchange.* National Area
    Development Institute, 1 January 1973, Lexington, Kentucky.
26. Shaffer, Ronald. 1972. The net economic impact of new industries on
    rural communities in eastern Oklahoma. Unpublished Ph.D. thesis.
    Stillwater: Department of Agricultural Economics, Oklahoma State Uni-
    versity.
27. Tweeten, Luther. 1973. Research resources for micropolitan develop-
    ment. In *Rural development: Research priorities.* North Central Re-
    gional Center for Rural Development. Ames: Iowa State Univ. Press.
28. ———. 1972. Manpower implications of the rural development act of
    1972. In *Manpower planning for jobs in rural America.* East Lansing:
    Center for Rural Manpower and Public Affairs, Michigan State Univer-
    sity.
29. Tweeten, Luther, and Lu, Yao-chi. 1973. Attitudes as a measure of op-
    timal place of residence. Paper presented to Midcontinent Regional Sci-
    ence Association (mimeo). Stillwater: Oklahoma State University.
30. Tweeten, Luther, and Ray, Daryll. Impact of public compensation poli-
    cies. In *Externalities in the transformation of agriculture.* Center for
    Agricultural and Rural Development. Ames: Iowa State Univ. Press.
    (Forthcoming).
31. Wadsworth, H. A., and Conrad, J. M. 1965. Leakages reducing employ-
    ment and income multipliers in labor surplus areas. *J. Farm Econ.*
    47:1,197–202.
32. Weber, Bruce. 1973. Trickling down: The responsiveness of rural poor
    family income and labor supply to regional economic growth. Unpub-
    lished Ph.D. thesis. Madison: University of Wisconsin.
33. Weisbrod, Burton. 1964. *External benefits of public education: An
    economic analysis.* Princeton, N.J.: Princeton Univ. Press.

CHAPTER NINE

ENHANCING SOCIAL OPPORTUNITY

HAROLD R. CAPENER

WHEN BACKING OFF to take a long look at the problem of social opportunity, one is impressed that the issue has more depth than meets the eye. Processes associated with all the life experiences from birth to death reflect on the social opportunities a person experiences. If it is true that we are products of our experiences, then our social opportunities become powerful predisposing forces in our lives.

One can view the problem of social opportunity through the eyes of the individual as the unit of analysis and argue that the perceptions and meanings the individual internalizes are what in the final analysis is important [17]. A second approach would utilize a social systems frame of reference and argue that individuals live out virtually all their lives in group level settings and that it is out of these settings that social opportunities derive their meaning [15, 21].

Each of these two ways of approaching the topic will take one in a substantively different direction, yet obviously each approach is an integral part of the other. For purposes of this chapter, I will focus on the second approach.

Two major issues are immediately raised by the chapter title, namely, the nature of social opportunity, and the nature of stable and/or declining communities. I will define social opportunity as the range of options available for individuals to enhance the quality and meaning of their lives in the context of their physical, social, economic, and psychological interactions.

The major issues in life imply the issues of living and participating in established institutions of communities—namely, to have access to: (1) a job and economic livelihood to provide an income sufficient for adequate diet and participation in other institutions; (2) quality

HAROLD R. CAPENER is Chairman, Department of Rural Sociology, Cornell University.

educational facilities for oneself and one's family, including the "intelligence" from mass media and "continuing education"; (3) health services, including an adequate water supply and sewage disposal as well as clinics, hospitals, and physicians; (4) other government services, including police, justice, and fire protection; (5) general and special shopping services; and (6) an infrastructure of voluntary organizations, both "instrumental" ones to assist in seeking these objectives, as well as "expressive" ones to assist in the enjoyment of life.

Enhanced social opportunities, then, mean that people have increasing rather than declining options, and/or access to such options, in any or all of the above institutional areas.

The second major issue, the nature of stable and/or declining communities and indeed whether people in these communities actually have fewer options, is somewhat more difficult to assess. I was struck by a statement made by Larson [14] that—excluding the excellent census work as illustrated by Beale and his associates—researchers probably know less about American rural society as it is today than they knew about our nation's rural life in the 1920s, 30s, and 40s. We may have a lot of information but we seemingly possess very little knowledge about what to do with it.

In point of fact, on certain key issues we do not have adequate information, for instance, on the access (or change in access) of people in rural communities to most of the above social institutions. Although we do know that the data are available "somewhere," at present they are neither readily nor systematically available. Using secondary sources, the Data Bank for Social Accounting in the Department of Rural Sociology at Cornell University has finally now amassed the capability for making assessments for most of New York State communities over 2,500 people and/or for the 300 Northeast U.S. counties for 1950, 1960, and 1970 [7]. But it has taken seven years and almost $100,000 to do this job, and it is still incomplete. Data are badly needed for the United States as a whole in order to answer some of these basic informational questions upon which further knowledge can be generated.

Since we do not know for certain about the nature of declining and stable rural communities, the next section is devoted to examining some of these issues. Then we will look briefly at some of the policy alternatives for declining and stable communities, and at some of the alternatives for state and federal policies in light of our examination.

CHANGES IN THE SOCIAL ORGANIZATION OF RURAL PLACES. What major evidence and principles regarding communities in decline are recognized today? The first principle seems to be that although many rural communities are stable or declining in population size (change in population size being a convenient if sometimes misleading index of enhanced or reduced social opportunities), the majority of rural counties are actually gaining in population. In the Northeast, for instance, only 31 percent of the 300 counties lost population between 1960 and 1970. Of these 134 were rural and of the rural 35 percent declined. Over half, 55 percent, of the rural counties were from the single state of West Virginia.

What appears to be happening is illustrated in the principle of form following function. Social opportunities have followed the shifting functions of transportation, communication, trade, and services. This process of opportunity following function has been amply documented since the turn of the century during the decades in which the form of communities experienced their greatest change. A description of the relationship between form and function in the development of Iowa communities illustrates this concept [8].

> In Iowa, county boundaries were established more than a century ago. County seat towns were centrally located within each county in order that any resident could journey to the county seat, transact his business and return home within the same day. A dense network connected the county seats and hence enhanced their economic position. Furthermore, many new towns sprang up along the railroads. Earlier settlements bypassed by the railroads decayed. Since 1885 few farms in Iowa have been more than six to eight miles from a railroad, grain elevator, and a town or village.
>
> Well before 1900 the size of banks, grocery stores, clothing stores, creameries, schools and churches were also determined against the background of travel by wagon over poor roads. Farm families did a large part of their shopping in villages of less than 1,000 people, and the four corners of the county felt little competition with one another or with the county seat.

Fuguitt also traces the changing relationships between the city and countryside in four areas: (1) transportation and communications; (2) trade, institutional, and social relationships; (3) occupational structure; and (4) population [9]. In the first area, Fuguitt points out that early concepts defining the country community in terms of the team haul have been transformed from the team wagon haul to the station wagon haul [24]. A comparison of figures demonstrates this change, for in 1921, of the approximately 3 million miles of rural roads, 13 percent were surfaced. But by 1959, this total had risen to 69 percent.

The trends of specialization reveal an increased overlapping relationship between trade centers and larger service areas [12]. The number of one-room schools in the nation as a whole dropped from 148,000 in 1930 to 75,000 in 1948 and to 26,000 in 1958. Similarly, the number of school districts dropped from 127,000 in 1932 to 42,000 in 1960 [19].

What appears to be happening in this situation may be set down in a second principle of rural social organization—that as profits in agriculture for marginal farmers decline and people move to nonfarm occupations, rural populations tend to move: (1) toward the most viable or growing centers in their own county; or, (2) toward more viable or growing centers in adjacent counties. The population redistributes itself both within a given county and between counties, but at the same time both counties and their major population centers grow in size and complexity. In fact, unpublished analyses by Moore, Taietz, and Young on the relationships of county seats and non-county-seat towns to institutional differentiation and complexity clearly demonstrate the county seats are generally the most viable type of rural community for further growth [18].

This pattern of population redistribution is not new but has simply become more intensified in recent decades. In his early comparative studies of the status of decline or stability of villages between 1900–1920, Brunner [5] noted that:

> The village in the United States taken by and large is not declining. Individual villages have declined but the trend has been toward an increasing population except where villages are very close together. . . . Here especially since the advent of the automobile and hard surfaced road it appears there are too many villages. . . . Two villages in every five have remained virtually stationary in the last two census periods.

Studies of the area around Ithaca, New York, provide excellent comparative data on the emergence, decline, and reemergence on a rural trade area just outside a county seat growth center. Ithaca's terrain is characterized by broad fertile valleys, smooth lower slopes, and steep infertile upper slopes; and its historical roots date back to revolutionary war times. As the expansion movement got underway, typical settlement enterprises included sawmills, gristmills, blacksmith shops, grocery stores, general stores, cheese factories, wagon shops, woolen mills, and hotels. Dairying, general farming, and some poultry were the main farming occupations.

The dominant growth in the area came in the late 1800s, and by 1900 the peak of growth had been reached. Farms were being abandoned, the population was shifting, and economic services were being discontinued.

But the 25-year period of 1926–1951 saw another shift in the development of the area outside Ithaca, and communities in decline began again to show signs of revitalization [3]. First, the population increased by 52 percent, rising from 1,495 in 1926 to 2,275 in 1951. The overall age composition was on an average three years younger in

1951, and the percent of population in the production years (20–49 years) rose from 33 percent to 41 percent during the 25-year span.

Furthermore, the area became a family residential center with more young families, more young persons per household, and fewer widows or widowers. Forty-three percent of the families living in the area in 1951 had been residents for less than five years. More of the adult male population were gainfully employed and significantly more of the adult females were working. The chief occupational pursuits in the area shifted from agriculture to skilled, semiskilled, unskilled, and clerical work with a marked increase in the latter category. Over three-fourths of the gainfully employed males and nearly 60 percent of the gainfully employed women worked outside of the Ithaca area, a distance of 4 to 12 miles away. Nearly three-fourths of the non-farming families lived on a place of one or more acres, thus enjoying the advantages of rural living while having proximity to the advantages of urban facilities.

Transportation and communication have transformed earlier factors of isolation. Ninety percent of the families own one or more automobiles, 80 percent live on hard surfaced roads while only 2 percent live on dirt roads. By 1951 communication services such as radios, newspapers, and mail delivery were found to cover virtually the entire area. Telephones were found in 57 percent of the homes compared to 48 percent in 1926.

The dominant pattern of informal social relations show them to be still centered at the locality level. Family visiting and sharing meals were the most popular forms, together with other social gatherings.

Only seven formal organizations surveyed in 1926 were still in existence in 1951. Four of these were extension organizations, two were lodges, and one was a grange. The more formal patterns of participation were carried out in organizations forming after 1926. Examples were volunteer fire departments, ladies fire department auxiliaries, sportsmen's clubs, Boy Scout troops, 4-H Clubs, memorial associations, community councils, and Parent-Teacher Associations. While in 1926, 32 percent of the families had no membership in any organizations, by 1951 this figure had been reduced to 11 percent.

The increased population, higher mobility, higher participation, and development of organizations to meet the needs of the men, women, and children indicate the outer Ithaca area had a higher degree of social opportunity than the previous 25 years. Further updating indicates that the area has continued on the same symbiotic pattern of close growth-center–suburban relationship characterizing other urbanizing areas. Virtually all of the available homes, especially farm homes with acreage, have been purchased by faculty or other professional or skilled workers in Ithaca. This county seat community, therefore, serves as the planning and nerve center tying a series of reasonably viable rural residential villages together for higher order services.

In a larger regional context, Ithaca sits in the middle of a triangle of three large metropolitan cities—Syracuse, Binghamton, and Elmira—each within a 50-mile radius. The prognosis for the villages within the triangle has to be optimistic as demand for rural residential living is everywhere apparent. This pattern seems to be characteristic of much of the Northeast.

Are such patterns viable for other areas of the United States? The problems of declining rural villages in the Great Plains do not allow for an equally optimistic prognosis. A study of Adams County, Nebraska, and six other similar counties [1, 2] indicates that the smaller trade centers cannot expect to supply more than day-to-day needs since the rural shopping patterns are shifting to the larger centers. Just as in the previously mentioned situation in Iowa, the Plains region is overcrowded with small service centers. Given today's transportation and communication technology, the centers represent uneconomic duplication of facilities.

Hodge [11] substantiates the above statements by four predictions from his study of sizes of trade centers by class of services in the three Canadian regions of Saskatchewan, Eastern Ontario, and Prince Edward Island:

> The number of farm trade centers will continue to decline as increases occur in farm size and farm mechanization, thereby lowering the man-land ratio and the market potential for grade center establishments.
>
> Hamlets will satisfy most daily shopping needs, and convenience centers will be bypassed by rural people seeking centers with a wider range of specialized goods and services. Convenience centers will decline to hamlet status in most instances and many present hamlets will disappear.
>
> Except for a limited amount of "suburbanization" around large cities, small trade centers will likely disappear within a radius of ten miles of large trade centers and will show substantial decline in areas up to fifteen miles away. Only beyond this distance is the trade area integrity of small centers likely to remain secure.
>
> As thinning out of small centers continues, rural people will have to travel as much as one-third farther to reach a center offering even day-to-day necessities. Higher-order centers will tend to emerge in a more regularly spaced pattern to serve the demands created by expanded farm incomes and the ability to exercise greater choice because of increased mobility.

Thus, although some writers [13] feel that decline of population in the rural communities inevitably leads to ineffective social organization—particularly in the ability of local hamlets and villages to provide schools, hospitals, and roads—we suggest that more inclusive units (counties, regions) be examined for population redistribution before evaluating a region's access to social opportunities.

Such considerations lead to a third general principle regarding rural social organization—that, despite relative growth of many rural regions over time, the levels of access to the type of institutional services denoting social opportunities generally do not match the access to such services in metropolitan or suburban areas. The issue is not necessarily one of growth or decline but rather that more differentiated and complex services tend to be located in larger urban centers. Hence, the people in rural regions tend to be "relatively deprived" in comparison with their urban counterparts.

For instance, the researchers of CSRS NE47 [20] have shown that poverty levels are both higher in rural compared to urban, suburban, or metropolitan areas, and that per capita welfare payments are lower. Similarly, Eberts has shown that rural counties in New York have fewer services than other types of counties and that the differences in comparisons over time are either stable or increasing [6]. To generalize these findings, although growth and decline in rural counties may be less of a problem, the relative deprivation in access to services in rural areas is still a problem. We should also point out that the "trade off" between lower costs for basic necessities in rural areas and transportation costs for access to these urban services is an important but largely unexamined area of analysis.

Policy Alternatives for Declining and Stable Counties or Regions.
The major policy issues facing decision makers at the local, regional, state, and federal levels regarding rural regions are to discover why rural regions are relatively deprived, and to discover how to resolve these discrepancies in order that people in rural areas can have the equalities which are their due (equalities to "life, liberty, and the pursuit of happiness").

Many people have commented on why the inequalities exist. In essence, the growth of goods and services depends upon, as Stein in *Eclipse of Community* points out, industrialization, bureaucratization, and urbanization [23]. Dispersed and low density populations apparently do not make an adequate population base for growth in services [4]. Moreover, people in rural areas who have money for investment apparently find greater returns by investing in urban and suburban places rather than in rural places. These investors shift capital resources out of their communities, and actually contribute to making urban places "more attractive" for their own young people. Such a paradox of values—the one of "family, home, and the rural good life" and the other of "return on investment" and the negative relation between them—probably seldom is seen by rural investors in their daily lives (perhaps because the "lags" in the correlations are too long).

Gouldner [10] comments on the declining old contexts and describes the shifting basis of the new economic political leverage:

> The educated bureaucratically employed, and highly mobile middle classes have a dwindling localistic attachment and a narrowing base of power on the local levels, which could provide them with the economic and political leverage to effectuate urban reform. They must in consequence seek a remedy not on the local level but on a national level. . . . Social reform now becomes a kind of engineering job, a technological task to be subject to bland "cost-benefit" or "system analysis." The rise of the welfare state then means the rise of reform at a distance. Reform today is no longer primarily a part-time avocation of dedicated amateurs but is increasingly the full-time career of paid bureaucrats.

In any case, even suggested reforms to such a "system" become remote from rural areas and from localistic concerns so that people feel the "big government bureaucracies" of "liberal reform" tend to be the only, but disliked, policy realities [16]. Rural people, therefore, tend to distrust these "solutions."

On the other hand, such federal "reforms" have also tended to support growth of state and local governments through "categorical matching funds" allocations. Growth of local governments in county seats is the largest sector of governmental growth and is at least in part attributable to such "revenue sharing" redistribution programs.

A major issue in creating policies for enhancing social opportunities through rural development is to create "working" models (ones which are testable, are empirically supported, and have policy implications) in order to direct policy decisions. Eberts and his associates in CSRS NE47 believe they are close to meeting these criteria [20]. They, along with a great many others (such as Fuguitt [9]), posit that rural regions increase in population size and services as the regions become better linked to urban and metropolitan political economies through such things as economic enterprises, government agencies, transportation systems, and communication facilities. These facilities provide new income to areas, but they also disturb local political economic power structures by bringing new information (greater fluidity) into the area. Such new information gives more people new ideas on how local community problems can be more satisfyingly resolved. Hence, local people might invest in new services or take advantage of latent services. In any event, they tend to learn to cope with their social and physical environments in more satisfying ways.

Although the research group [20] in NE47 have not completed their work, they do note that each variable in their model is policy-manipulable by authorities at state and federal levels. For instance, all types of linkages are federally subsidized, services are part and parcel of government programs, and "fluidity" (or information exchange) is the essence of things like educational institutions and cooperative extension. The study design, by the way, is concerned with macrostructural variables (i.e., the forms of relationship between the units in the system such as centralized, decentralized, or many sources of information in areas versus "single" sources of information). It is assumed that the patterns of relations of macrostructural variables (linkages, differentiation, fluidity) are more directly associated with causal variables of change than more traditional aggregate variables (i.e., the characteristics of units in the system such as age, median income, or sex ratios) and also cause social opportunities more than traditional aggregate variables. A second consideration is that the macrostructural level and the system level problems are the kinds of problems that need to be addressed to influence the future of villages, communities, and regions.

This type of macrostructural system level analysis would seem to hold real promise in its potential for searching out the kinds of discriminating variables significantly associated with growth or decline and for providing the necessary policy oriented intelligence data for planning and coping with such phenomena.

A highly imaginative national design to experiment with various strategy approaches to rural development in Canada (which also relates to the above thinking) represents a second innovative approach in specifying resolutions to rural regional problems. Large sums were allocated to be spent within the single "poorest" county in each of six Canadian provinces. In the Province of New Brunswick, the development strategies undertaken in Kent County have been largely guided by the NE47 type of system level macrostructural research to identify which problems and policy issues might have payoff potential [22].

The county chosen for intensive treatment here had all of the characteristics of rural decline, depletion, and despondency. New Brunswick Newstart was composed of a team of researchers and action workers devoted to evaluating the adequacy of the general model (similar to the one described above for NE47) for a single county and set of rural communities, and assisting people in creating and taking advantage of local opportunities for social and economic development. The team was composed of a group of social scientists—three economists, three sociologists, two psychologists, one home economist, one educator—together with a group of local residents, all under 40, taken from the ranks of the locally unemployed, and retrained as paraprofessionals These paraprofessionals were to give and receive relevant information from other local people and were sent into the rural communities of Kent County to seek such information for processing on evaluation and feasibility. Whenever possible, the social scientists worked closely with the local residents in resolving their problems.

After four years in a five-year experiment, the following propositions were postulated as essentially correct for Kent County and are important for further analysis elsewhere:

1. The assumption that urban investments have more economic efficiency returns than do rural investments needs to be seriously re-examined at a more total system level.
2. There is positive evidence that rural investments have higher per capita multiplier benefits than urban investments.
3. Rural investments are generally less costly and return higher yields on investment given equivalent management components.
4. Management in rural areas needs some outside support in new techniques from time to time (such as from a Newstart team of social scientists), because on their own most such communities cannot afford such services. These services, with a lag, however, can become cost effective.
5. The most serious limitation to appropriate adjustments in rural areas is one of expectations and understanding rather than physical or economic constraints.
6. The limitations of expectations and understanding are largely man-made and therefore can be significantly altered.
7. Most of the significant decision processes affecting the personal lives of individuals and the collective lives of families, groups, organizations, institutions, and communities are made with too little examination or access to potential alternatives.
8. Econometric models will yield better policy intelligence if thorough-going input-output analysis is carried on down through the small units of analysis (e.g., by examining the potential impact of the construction of a large hospital at a new point in a rural region in terms of employment and support services such as laundry, restaurant, motel, etc.). The notion here is to effectively tie social organization planning to physical planning.
9. Employing trained planning and development leaders along with paraprofessionals to work closely and carefully with public and private leaders, groups, and organizations to enhance the flow of information, knowledge, ideas, and alternatives for action which may be necessary in order to produce viable resolutions to local opportunities. For example, in the first year of operation, 90 suggestions were identified in a series of small group meetings to survey actions that might be feasible. Not one of the 90 were acted upon, but over two years, a new list of 20 viable projects grew out of the discussions and interactions.
10. Communications, interaction, and correlation are the capital

stock for enhancing social opportunities. In many ways these are the least expensive of the inputs, yet have promise of highest yields on viable outputs for development.

11. The current stocks of folklore and local intelligence are most systematically processed (and exploited) by contractors, realtors, and other commercial speculators who generally are nonresidents. New combinations of private, public, semiprivate, semipublic collectivities need to be formulated to tinker with the technical and social machinery to come out with better performance standards for benefits to local people.

12. It is demonstrably feasible to do action research in rural development where action derives from research.

13. There is great utility in experimenting with a pilot, in-depth county in order to test the models, test various techniques for reality, and explore the feasibility of maximizing the expansion components.

14. A strong interdisciplinary team of three to five professionals who are public employees are needed to start the ball rolling. They need a lead time of approximately 18 months without pressure for accountability. Significant results should not be expected until the end of the third or fourth year.

15. It is important in the process to involve large numbers of people in meetings, discussions, and forums. The result is that people meet others from different backgrounds in diverse settings. New ideas, combinations, and options are generated that otherwise would never arise.

16. It is the responsibility of the professional leadership to help make the hard decisions with respect to project feasibilities, priorities, what will work and pay off, and what won't.

The essence of these considerations on population redistribution and on the two sets of projects is to indicate that local development is possible. Rural people are losing opportunities because the market patterns of the society in which they exist do not support such local initiatives. Yet when New Brunswick Newstart leaves, Kent County will have 300 new permanent jobs—indigenously created (not by enticing large firms to locate there)—on the base of barely 7,000 previously employed, and new income of about $1 million per year (not counting local multipliers).

Moreover, policies at the local, state, and federal levels can assist in such development. Two problems exist here: (1) the exact models for such development need further refinement through research (such as asking, "what is the minimum staff for optimum effect in which type of county structure?"), and (2) such development operates only with a time lag. Sismondo of New Brunswick Newstart estimates that the start-up time is no less than 18 months, and that positive results take a minimum of three years [22].

Finally, the social opportunities "enhanced" by this work (especially New Brunswick Headstart) include everything from creating new jobs (both on the basis of cooperatives and of private enterprise) to assisting mothers on welfare through classes on child-rearing, nutrition, homemaking, and house remodeling. A major result is that the people assisted by the project (and interestingly, others in their communities, too) are, as a social category, more independent and autonomous in their decision making, less alienated, less given to psychosomatic symptoms, and have more income, better facilities, and, in general, greater personal and collective capacities and capabilities [22]. These results may not constitute what everyone deems social opportunities, but they would seem to catch at least part of what everyone believes them to be. Social opportunities have been influenced by conscious policy manipulation of key variables.

CONCLUSIONS. Evidence has been amply documented that social opportunities in declining communities are heavily influenced by the factors of size, density, rate, and duration of the period of decline. It must be accepted that just as many villages and hamlets have experienced demise in the past, still others are destined to share the same fate in the future. The question then is not whether some communities will grow or decline but under what circumstances, with what consequences, and with what degrees of inevitability given certain alternative choices of change intervention.

Since change as a process is always at work undercutting established patterns, whether the community is expanding or declining is of great importance. In an expanding community, the alternatives in reestablishing and maintaining successive degrees of equilibrium are optimized. In a declining community the options are reduced, and the aura of the social climate has the feel of a losing cause. The psychological effect weighs heavily on all facets of planning and decision making on the part of individuals, groups, organizations, agencies, and institutions.

An interesting anomaly is readily seen in the declining agrarian rural community. It is the contrast between acceptance of and accommodation to change in the life system of the farm family and the agribusiness support structure and the rejection of change in the community structure. Farming is based on the phenomenon of changing seasons, growing of crops, and animal breeding. Our very livelihood depends on these changes. Change is also present in the social processes of altering family compositions through marriage, establishment of new homes, and the birth of children. These dramatic changes tend to be reduced to the ordinary and are naturally accommodated. How is it, then, that physical and social change of such dynamic character can be depended on and lived by in one sector, the life system of the farm, but resisted and little understood in the larger life system of the community?

Seemingly, the deficiency of understanding changes lies in the frame of reference. The mind's eye of citizens in communities is inadequately trained to see and respond flexibly. Though we live by change, there are components of it which we intuitively resist. We are never prepared for our communities to grow old and obsolete, just as we are not prepared to grow old and obsolete ourselves.

A feasible alternative is to employ some new strategies to combat declining change. This alternative first requires abandoning the position of attempting to resist or ignore the reality of the change. The good old days will never be again, and the truth is they probably never were. Secondly, new alliances, new combinations, consolidations, and consortiums will need to be explored. The tradeoff here is that of time and distance as influenced by the mobility of the farm wagon compared to the family station wagon.

Yet, in an age when time-distance factors are being reduced, social opportunities must be conceived as extending beyond neighborhood to county and region. However, in so doing, opportunities for a locality must not be lost in large scale system analysis. For there is no way that the small social unit of the family can effectively interact with the larger units of the state, region, or nation. Only through his own ecological position in the community structure can the individual engage in meaningful interaction [25]. It is primarily within this context that his social opportunities will be realized—that the quality of his life will have its real meaning.

REFERENCES

1. Anderson, A. H. 1953. The changing role of the small town in farm areas. Lincoln: Nebraska Agricultural Experiment Station Bulletin 419.
2. ———. 1961. The "expanding" rural community. Lincoln: Nebraska Agricultural Experiment Station Bulletin 5B464.
3. Anderson, W. A., Larson, O. F., and Falloul, A. S. 1956. Social change in the Slaterville Springs-Brooktondale area of Tompkins County, New York, 1926–1951. Ithaca: New York State Agricultural Experiment Station Bulletin.
4. Berry, Brian. 1960. *Essays on geography and economic development.* Chicago: Univ. of Chicago Press.
5. Brunner, Edward deS. 1927. *Village communities.* New York: George H. Doran Co.
6. Eberts, Paul R. 1972. Consequences of changing social organization in the northeast. In *Papers of the workshop on current rural development regional research in the northeast.* Ithaca, N.Y.: Northeast Regional Center for Rural Development, Cornell University.

7. Erickson, Eugene C., Carruthers, Garrey E., and Oberle, Wayne H. 1972. Institutional structures for improving rural community services. In *Papers of the workshop on current rural development regional research in the northeast.* Ithaca, N.Y.: Northeast Regional Center for Rural Development, Cornell University.
8. Fox, Karl A. 1962. The study of interaction between agriculture and the nonfarm economy: Local, regional, and national. *J. Econ.* 64:16.
9. Fuguitt, Glenn V. 1963. City and countryside. *Rural Soc.* 28:248.
10. Gouldner, Alvin F. 1968. The sociologist as partisan: Sociology and the welfare state. *Am. Soc.* 3:103–16.
11. Hodge, Gerald. 1965. Do villages grow? Some perspectives and predictions. *Rural Soc.* 31:195.
12. Kolb, John H. 1969. *Emerging rural communities.* Madison: Univ. of Wisconsin Press.
13. Kraenzel, Carl F. 1955. *The Great Plains in transition.* Norman: Univ. of Oklahoma Press.
14. Larson, Olaf F. 1973. Sociological research problems. In *Rural development: Research priorities.* Ames: Iowa State Univ. Press.
15. Loomis, Charles P. 1960. *Social systems: Essays on their persistence and change.* Princeton, N.J.: Van Nostrand Co.
16. Lowi, Theodore. 1969. *The end of liberalism.* New York: W. W. Norton.
17. Meade, George Herbert. 1938. *The philosophy of the act.* Chicago: Univ. of Chicago Press.
18. Moore, Dan E., Taietz, Philip, and Young, F. W. 1973. The location of institutions in upstate New York. Ithaca, N.Y.: Dept. of Rural Sociology Bulletin, College of Agriculture and Life Sciences, Cornell University.
19. Noble, M.S.C., Jr. and Dawson, Howard A. 1961. *Handbook of rural education.* Washington, D.C.: Department of Rural Education of the National Education Association for the United States.
20. Northeast Regional Center for Rural Development. 1972. NE47 consequences of changing social organization in the northeast. In *Papers of the workshop on current rural development regional research in the northeast.* Ithaca, N.Y.: Northeast Regional Center for Rural Development, Cornell University.
21. Parsons, Talcott. 1951. *The social system.* Glencoe, Ill.: Free Press.
22. Sismondo, Sergio. 1973. *Applications of structural indicators for the measurement of development: Selected findings for rural communities in Kent County.* New Brunswick, Canada: New Brunswick Newstart.
23. Stein, Maurice R. 1960. *The eclipse of community: An interpretation of American studies.* Princeton, N.J.: Princeton Univ. Press.
24. Wilson, Warren H. 1912. *The evolution of the country community.* New York: Pilgrim Press.
25. Young, Ruth C., and Larson, Olaf F. 1970. The social ecology of a rural community. *Rural Soc.* 35:337–53.

CHAPTER TEN

FEASIBLE OPTIONS FOR SOCIAL ACTION

GEORGE DONOHUE

ABOUT EVERY 25 years, we redis-
cover the poor in America and also
lament the demise of the quality of life in rural areas. There have
been exhortations from federal, state, and local politicians; farm and
industrial leaders; and scholars suggesting that the very fabric of the
nation is threatened unless something is done to halt the senseless
piling up of people in our cities and the consequent decline in population density and quality of human services in our rural areas. A
cursory examination of the history of federal programs shows numerous attempts to stem the tide of urban migration. These programs
rely primarily on investment efforts intended to encourage relocation
or maintain employment in rural areas in view of the declining need
for farm labor. The persistence of the urban movement in the face
of these programs, as well as the continued exhortations, attest to the
limited success of those efforts.

EARLY ORIENTATION. Conferences on development and the reports of the National Food and Fiber Commission and the National Advisory Commission on Rural Poverty continually pursue remedies to the problems associated with rural people and their
social organization. Until the early 1960s most of the programs of
social action were related to a reaffirmation of the life-style and values
associated with small autonomous communities and individual enterprise on Main Street as well as on the family farm. This form of
social organization was deemed desirable as an ideal format in which
human development and expression could be maximized. It was also

G. A. DONOHUE is Professor of Sociology, University of Minnesota.

felt to be the best form for providing a most fertile condition for the largest return from the nation's agricultural resources. Given this position, any attempt to provide programs that would basically alter the social organization of rural America were frowned upon and considered undesirable and therefore not feasible courses of social action.

A growing array of evidence during the 1950s and early 1960s indicated that however qualitatively good the life-style of the small rural community organization might have been, metropolitan areas continued to grow and began to reproduce. At the same time, objective indices related to quality of life such as education, medical services, libraries, and other such criteria indicated that the small community format with declining population, a shrinking economic base, and a changing age composition was unable to maintain competitive standards associated with a quality of life being experienced in the larger, more densely populated urban centers.

CHANGING ORIENTATIONS. Since the early 1960s, increasing attention has been focused on the problem of how one goes about inducing change to bring about a transition from emphasis upon small, independent, autonomous communities (inhabited by individuals with the social skills associated with the consensus type of social organization and with the belief that independence is born largely of self-sufficiency) to a social organization format based primarily upon pluralism and diversity (with a population trained in the skills of conflict accommodation and with a mind-set embodying the idea that independence is born of interdependence). This appears to have been a major task in and of itself, but it may be nearly impossible to accomplish it and not appear to be defaulting on an earlier obligation to maintain the status quo in the format of rural social organization. One might even suggest that social action programs designed to reformulate the social organization of rural areas in this fashion and which are presented to appear as a reaffirmation of the old order are at best deceptive.

It would perhaps be more honest and of considerable help in focusing on feasible alternatives if we issued a forthright statement indicating that however useful the format of early community organization in rural America was, it has in large measure had a diminishing utility and for all practical purposes is obsolete as a form of social technology. The early rural community in some respects bears the same relationship to modern community organization that open pit mining bears to taconite processing in northern Minnesota. The obsolescence of the traditional rural format implies the obsolescence of roles as well as skills associated with those roles, just as is true of the open pit mining operations.

The obsolescence of the rural community, its inability to function effectively, and the trained incapacity of skills represented therein is best stated in Chapter 10, "Area and Regional Development," of *The People Left Behind*.[1] The National Commission emphatically recommends that regional and areawide social structures be created and coordinated on a state and national basis. It also recommends that social action be instituted to result in comprehensive planning, utilizing professional staffs for problem definition, and program implementation. This has become the feasible option for social action in dealing with the problems of rural America.

While much literature in social organization indicates that regional or areawide development organizations derive their basic impetus from the needs generated by national and state concerns for coordinated and interdependent development, there is some belief that this structure emerges from needs of the local community. It would appear that it is an attempt to allow the insufficient social technology of the local community to meet the needs of people. In many respects, regional organizations, in order to be effective, must have an impact upon the traditional sovereignty assumed by the rural community. If the regional format is to have any appreciable impact upon increasing the quality of life available to persons currently residing in communities left behind, it is quite evident that local concerns will take precedence over regional concerns only in matters that are basically insignificant in the life-style of most persons. Therefore, feasible social options are basically related to factors beyond control of the local community.

Regionalization is the most feasible social option for a number of reasons, but two are basic: (1) it is evident that the current format of local organization is inadequate to provide the services and funding compatible with current standards of living in the larger system, and (2) that regionalization and comprehensive planning have been anointed on both federal and state levels as the pattern of organization most compatible with the requirements for social control of human behavior consistent with goal attainment in the larger system. In view of the second condition, the power relationship between the local community and the state and federal governments make any confrontation unlikely. In spite of the above, there will be tremendous social costs associated with the struggle to maintain the status quo on the part of local leaders and residents.

While regionalization may appear as a panacea to some individuals, as well as the most feasible option for social action for the reasons cited, a few precautionary notes about the problems and consequences of regionalization should be mentioned.

1. *The People Left Behind,* U.S. National Advisory Commission on Rural Poverty, U.S. Government Printing Office, 1967.

REGIONALISM AND DEVELOPMENT. Even a cursory examination of recent history of governmental organization would indicate the acceptance of regionalization as an accomplished fact.[2] Minnesota, as has every other state in the union, has been encouraged with various types of incentives to establish regional divisions in order to be eligible for various federal programs. While in most instances a region does not have to be established, the federal government expects an equivalent organizational structure to be eligible for participation in most federal programs. From the purely administrative standpoint, it seems quite clear that the "span of control," a notion that no more than 15 units be responsible to any one unit as a principle of management, is a guiding criterion in determining the overall number of regions nationally and statewide. However arbitrary this may seem to lay persons, the majority of professionals in the area of social organization and administration would accept it as a reasonable guideline. In view of this criterion, it is not difficult to understand that one statehouse dealing with 11 regions rather than 87 counties would hypothetically be able to communicate more effectively and thus administrate programs more efficiently. It seems that a greater trend toward regionalization will be the predominant mode for organizations in the public and the private sectors in the years ahead.

While regionalization may be the accepted mode, everyone associated with its implementation has recognized that there are any number of problems to overcome before the ideal of an effective functioning region can be achieved. First, and not the least among these problems, is the social-psychological set of the resident population. An acceptance of the concept of regionalization requires both an intellectual understanding of interdependence and an emotional acceptance of the perspective that one's independence is a product of interdependence. The traditional mental set that is a part of the ideological heritage of our country as a whole, with particular emphasis in the rural farm sector, is the idea that independence is born of self-sufficiency or, at best, limited interdependence restricted to the family unit. While it is possible for large numbers of rural residents to harbor such a notion and operate as though it were true (witness many of the attitudinal surveys indicating the desire for self-employment among industrial workers in the metropolitan area), it is virtually impossible to have an effective regional leadership which continues to think within the constraints of the social-psychological model of rugged individualism.

The mental set of the rural population is reinforced by an orga-

---

2. Forty-four states have instituted regional structures, and the Advisory Commission on Intergovernmental Relations adopted recommendations at its June, 1973, meeting in San Francisco calling for stronger regions as a basis for more effective decision making. *Planning*, October, 1973, pp. 5–6.

nizational structure that tends to place a premium upon relative self-sufficiency within the rural community. The development of linkages with other communities is encouraged only where necessary as a condition for community survival. Thus, while interdependency exists among local communities at the present time, it should not necessarily be assumed that these linkages may provide a basis for escalating and building more complex linkages among the communities. In many cases where such linkages exist, they are a matter of gentlemen's agreements based upon interpersonal relationships and not upon principles of regional planning, integration, and interdependence. These linkages generally are a part of the power position of each of the personalities involved, and their continuation is dependent upon a perception of personal benefits derived by the power figures.

Inasmuch as current patterns of regionalization are not tied to the existing personalities in local power structures, they tend to threaten the status of power figures. In doing so, they also undermine the internal as well as external relationships of existing community structures that depend upon these interpersonal relationships.

Equally important from a structural standpoint is the fact that the traditional ideology is accompanied by what is known as a *consensus model* of social organization. This model is dependent upon general agreement among participants before any decision is made or action undertaken. The model of regionalization, in contrast, constitutes a *conflict model* of organization which recognizes that conflict will occur and that action must proceed without general agreement and be subject to considerable dispute in the process. Recent studies of the role of conflict in larger and smaller communities indicate quite clearly that the small communities tend to repress conflict and to forestall action when conflict occurs.[3]

Leadership skills required for operating within the context of a conflict model must be acquired just as leadership skills for a consensus model have been acquired by current social leaders in the smaller communities. Debriefing and reeducation is not often a short-term proposition and indeed in many cases a trained incapacity to respond to a new mode of social organization may be one of the greatest obstacles to its implementation of development via regional structures.

An effective case might be made for the idea that regional social organization allows for more effective communication and more efficient administration. However, it does not necessarily follow that regional social organization results in either relatively greater or lesser social power for the participating units, nor does it necessarily follow

3. Clarice N. Olien, George A. Donohue, and Phillip J. Tichener, "The Community Editor's Power and the Reporting of Conflict," *Journalism Quarterly*, 45(1968):243–52.

that there is either greater or lesser socioeconomic development. If the particular power or resource condition or quality of life of every region is related to its availability of resources, it may, through more effective internal organizations and more effective interorganizational relationships with other elements of the society, make an impact upon these conditions. However, it is equally possible that an area which is already relatively underdeveloped economically and politically may be in the same relative position after regional organization as it was before, provided equally effective regional structuring occurs in the more socially and politically affluent areas of the state. Given the general development of regions already cited, one might well expect this condition to exist. Thus the intervening variable of regional organization might have no impact or may have a negative impact in the sense that the gap in development between less affluent and more affluent regions of the state might grow disproportionately in favor of the more affluent areas as a consequence of regionalization. There is nothing in regionalization as an organizational form that would prevent the competition among regions from occurring as it does now among communities.

This last point brings up another consideration about regionalization: If regionalization is to live up to its full promise of social and economic development, is not national planning implicit within the regional concept? If national planning is a prerequisite to effective and perhaps equitable development, it would call for the implementation of a series of controls on the migration of populations, capital, and other resources. While regionalization may be an effective instrument of social development without extensive national planning, it would seem that its full potential would await a change in national values regarding the deployment of people and resources. The current climate in both rural and metropolitan areas is not conducive to the development and exercise of such extensive controls.

One of the outstanding aspects of traditional community organization has been the assumption that many of the functions could be and indeed should be performed by individuals without specialized training. Individuals with specialized skills or expertise have been considered relatively unnecessary if not inimical to democratic government in the small community. In the metropolitan areas, the role of the professional is essential to not only private corporate operations but also the the public corporate body. In what ways should the professional enter the decision making process? What responsibilities should the professional bear to his or her constituents? These are real questions associated with regional development in rural areas. One might argue that the regional development concept will make explicit not only the function but also the responsibility of the professional who is already operating in government circles. This might result in an increase in social responsibility and define the limits of the professional's decision making function beyond current constraints. Yet the point remains that in metropolitan areas which have utilized the principles associated with regional organization for a number of years, the problem of the role of the professional and/or the technician and their relationship to their clientele have not been adequately defined. This is particularly true in the area of professionals whose expertise lies in organization and planning. In the minds of many leaders in small communities, the question is not whether or not we will create a new elite or how that elite will control, but rather how the elite will be controlled.

A further consideration is that any organizational structure, that of the local community or that of the region, must, if it is to be successful as an organizational device, be able to predict and control the behavior of its participants. If both the quality and quantity of outcomes in terms of human behavior are to be highly predictable, then it becomes necessary to increase the control constraint in order to reduce deviations. Among the difficulties with this is that there is a tendency to move from social legislation which tends to stress a *"thou shalt not"* character to social legislation which tends to stress *"thou shalt"* requirements. That is, legislation similar to our current affirmative action programs. Unless there are only two alternative forms of behavior, it becomes obvious that such legislation tends to be in highly restrictive forms of social control, but such restriction is required if greater predictability and control is to be achieved to insure specific outcomes. Such legislation is not unique to the large-scale community and may be found in the small-scale community, but the tendency to move in this direction in large-scale organization is quite clear in the history of social legislation in our society.

The viability of any option for social action is dependent in large part upon the conditions of organization which impinge upon the particular option. A community choosing an option for action that is not consistent with the federal and state mandates for regional development faces a low probability of success. The low probability is not based on the substantive merit of the option, but rather on the contest of power between regional planning and individual community choice. The generally held assumption that a viable option for the community will also be viable for the region and vice versa is hardly valid. If that were the case the old laissez-faire system would suffice rather than regional structures engaged in purposive planning and direction.

In many respects the advice of the late Sam Rayburn, long-term Democratic Speaker of the House of Representatives, to individuals is appropriate for rural communities today, "To get along—go along."

The individual emotional costs as well as the group social and economic costs of nonregional alternatives will be extremely high.

One should not assume that to "go along" means to simply acquiesce to regional and other forces beyond the community. It could also mean active participation in regional forms of planning and decision making, giving the local community some voice in at least deciding what are feasible options for the region.

CHAPTER ELEVEN

FEASIBLE OPTIONS FOR ECONOMIC DEVELOPMENT

JOHN W. MAMER, L. T. WALLACE, AND GEORGE E. GOLDMAN

CALIFORNIA has an applied research-extension program for community leaders and public officials to facilitate economic evaluation of selected short-run options in rural development. The program, which has evolved since the early 1960s, had its beginnings in certain California agricultural extension programs of the early 1930s.

In the early 1960s our procedures were quite simple and traditional. We assembled economic information for use in working with local groups to gain an economic perspective of their situation. Then we assisted in organizing economic conferences to focus public attention and create discussion on problems and alternative solutions.

Communities with which we have worked include those with increasing population, static population, and decreasing population. In each case the composition of age, sex, education, and other parameters of the populace was different. Therefore, the local employment situation and demand for and supply of public services are different for each community. In a state as large and diverse as California, there are always communities in each of the three categories.

On a day-to-day basis a good part of our community resource development work is concerned with problem identification and specification. Our county staff includes this activity as part of their professional responsiblities. Statewide agricultural extension specialists are frequently involved in various stages of discussion with local leaders and interest groups, but the focus of attention remains on the local problem. The element of the program that I will center on in this chapter is the generation of information and analysis that

JOHN W. MAMER, L. T. WALLACE, and GEORGE E. GOLDMAN are Extension Economists, University of California, Berkeley.

relates predominantly to the economic appraisal of the alternatives facing the community.

Whatever the population situation, community leaders need detailed economic information regarding their community and the impacts likely to result from the pursuit of any given option. We provide a framework of analysis so that choices facing the community can be evaluated. Our experience suggests that the quality of local decision making about resource use can be improved if this is done.

The word "analytical" deserves emphasis since it draws attention to the interrelationship among variables—that is, how changes in one sector of the local economy are related to changes in each of the other sectors. This is elementary material for economists, but the analytical framework is valuable in determining the economic impact of the options available to the community.

This analytical framework is also valuable in making explicit the relationship of goals to options. A resource development program can rarely wait until all conflicts among goals are resolved, but careful consideration of goals is an integral part of the process of the search for and evaluation of options.

In our work we have found the following general goals widely held by leaders and residents of nonmetropolitan areas: (1) a desire to avoid a high population density, congestion, and other perceived ills of the "big city;" (2) a desire to avoid the hardships brought about by economic decline or stagnation; (3) a desire to keep or preserve a rural environment; and (4) a desire to be able to sell locally-held assets that are increasing in value

Accordingly, we feel our program has these objectives: (1) an accurate evaluation of the economic implications of various projects designed to achieve one or more of the above goals; (2) estimates of the costs and revenues to local government given alternative resource uses; and (3) identifying and analyzing possible conflicts in resource use in the community and alternative methods of resolving these conflicts.

EVOLUTION OF THE PROGRAM. We do not think that there is anything unique or optimal about our experience, yet it may be useful to trace briefly the evolution of our program. Through it, we came to accept the importance of analyzing the sectoral interrelationships of the local economy. By 1962 the effect of urban growth in agricultural areas was becoming quite evident. Accordingly, we organized a statewide conference on "Urban Growth in Agricultural Areas" and invited 200 agricultural and urban leaders from throughout the state. The main message we received from those who attended was that they wanted agricultural extension help in identifying feasible alternatives and in appraising their implications, but they wanted to be able to act according to local preferences.

Working with Napa County leaders in 1963, we organized the first of a series of county economic conferences. In November, 1965, we held a second conference in that county. In at least one county we have held three conferences, in some, two; in total we have held more than a dozen conferences, and more are still being organized.

At these conferences we presented economic and social data that described the "current" trends, some of which were clearly evident and some not so evident. However, the data presented were not such as to enable local people to answer "what" and "if" questions. This kind of question is typified by: What would happen to the economy of the area if agriculture declined by one-third? If industry doubled in volume? If all the premium wine grape land were converted to urban uses? When we ask the question what would happen, what we really mean as economists is: What would happen to each of the other sectors and to the total economy of the area? What would be the economic pattern of expansion or contraction?

INPUT-OUTPUT ANALYSIS. To answer these kinds of questions we needed a system of analysis that would describe the interrelationships that exist among sectors of the region's economy. That kind of analysis could be provided most easily by an input-output model of the region.

Fortunately, about that time we were able to partially finance a project from funds received under Title I of the Higher Education Act of 1965. Once we had funding, we selected, from among the areas with which we were working, a relatively self-contained region. The five counties north of San Francisco Bay, shown in Figure 11.1, met our requirements reasonably well. These counties have much in common, yet they have some dissimilarities, too. One common item is that premium wine grapes can be grown in four of the five counties.

Marin County is unique in being the northern gateway to San Francisco, and it has the heaviest exposure to San Francisco oriented commuter traffic. However, all five counties are subject to urbanizing influences, and all have a residential or recreational potential which has long been of interest to the urban Bay Area dwellers.

The collection of data is a crucial part of an input-output analysis, and it is also the most difficult, time consuming, and expensive part of the task. Obtaining the dollar flow, or transactions table, is the heart of the process. This table presents a monetary picture of the total volume of economic activity in the county. Once the dollar flow table is assembled, obtaining technical coefficients and the interdependence coefficients are routine matters. But before one

FIG. 11.1.   Counties included in the five-county project appear as shaded areas.

begins to collect data, the participatory process can be a vehicle for: (1) economic education; (2) involving leading citizens, public officials, and their staffs in a study of their community; and (3) laying a foundation for carrying on the work by local groups. We involved local leaders in decisions regarding the appropriate sectors into which to apportion their economy. In these same decisions we also worked closely with county agricultural extension staffs.

The role of the local extension staff was essential to the success of our project. They worked with us in constructing the model's agricultural sectors; they reviewed data and helped us adjust for differences among counties. As a by-product they substantially increased their knowledge about the local economy. They also were extremely helpful in securing cooperation and data from nonfarm businesses in their counties.

After we had completed assembly of the data, performed the necessary calculations, and prepared reports based on the research, we faced the second educational opportunity. We did not want the results of our work to end up in the bookcases of local units of government, read by no one. As implied at the beginning of this chapter, we did not view this research as a cure-all for the many difficulties the communities faced. However, we did think that it would be useful if this kind of systematic economic analysis could become part of local decision making machinery. This goal, as a minimum, required that the work receive public attention and some reading and discussion. Participants in that discussion would include ourselves and the extension staff, local leaders and government officials, and hopefully their staffs.

We worked with our local county agricultural extension staff in organizing several public meetings, one in each of the five counties, at which we presented the results of our input-output study. At these sessions we gave a simple explanation of the input-output model, carefully specifying its assumptions and limitations as well as its appropriate uses. We developed a set of hypothetical applications specific to each county illustrating the ways that input-output analysis is useful in providing quantitative information.

Following these public meetings, ranging in size from 100 to 150 participants, we met with local planning boards and other county officials in smaller groups to review the work's potential uses to them and to relate our analysis to other information available to them. In these smaller sessions the local agricultural extension office again played a key role. Out of these sessions came further requests for specific studies on issues the counties faced regarding mobil homes, county expenditures on local parks, closing of a state hospital, and other issues affecting the economic consequences of local resource use options.

We should elaborate more on the role of the county agricultural extension office. Jack Fiske, a county director who had an appreciation for the value of economic analysis in local decision making, was one of a few extension staff members in the counties who was trained as an economist. He received his master's degree in agricultural economics from Berkeley. Most county-based staff are trained in the natural sciences and therefore are most comfortable in natural science areas of decision making.

By involving local staff members in the project, we were able to provide an opportunity for some of them to expand their scope of interest. We also made them slightly more comfortable in an area of decision making that could take more of their time in the future.

Several events tended to highlight the effectiveness and usefulness of the input-output model in appraising the impact of economic change where the impending change was one of decline. In one county the state decided to close a state hospital which had 1,000 employees and an annual payroll of about $12 million. Local leaders wanted to appraise the impact of this decision on other sectors of the county's economy. After a few days of collecting data from officials of the hospital and county, we were able to give a quantitative estimate of the economic impact of the loss of the hospital compared with four other resource options. The result showed the high multiplier effect of the hospital compared to the others.

In another case, a dam was proposed that would have flooded a rather picturesque valley. Questions arose about the dam's economic implications. Using data assembled by an agricultural extension staff member, we appraised the impact of flooding the valley. This relatively small study was carried out primarily by a livestock farm advisor who became interested in the practicality of our analytic efforts. The results of his efforts were used by state officials in their decision to veto the dam's construction.

In another case, a late frost reduced the Napa County grape crop. After receiving appraisals of crop damage from local grape specialists, we were able to provide the county board of supervisors with estimates of the probable economic impact of the freeze the morning after it occurred. These estimates were helpful to the board in filing an application for disaster relief.

In another illustration, the input-output model provided us with a quantitative measure of the volume of business activity caused by visitors to Napa County's wineries. County officials and businessmen were surprised by the volume of business activity, both direct and indirect, generated by tourists.

FUTURE INPUT-OUTPUT WORK. While continuing to meet with county officials and staff members to help them use results of our study, we also are expanding the scope of our initial project to produce a generalized model adaptable to any of the state's counties. One goal of our program is to train county personnel to continue to update the data while we help mainly with expanding the range of economic analysis to new problems and issues. We also would like to see other analytical procedures influence local decision making. Of these procedures, simulation is an obvious candidate.

DECLINING COMMUNITY. In the previous section most of the illustrations of the use of our work pertained to economic events that indicated some degree of economic decline for the community. Our experience is about equally divided between declining and expanding situations, but requests for assistance in declining situations have more of a hint of emergency than do requests stemming from growth problems. This experience no doubt reflects (1) the greater difficulty of adjustment to change that is of a declining nature, and (2) the national consensus that growth is good and decline is bad.

It has been our experience that even in stable and declining communities, there is not a solid consensus regarding economic growth; the champion of "growth at any price" is no longer vocal. I do not want to imply that California and the country as a whole is not predominantly growth oriented. Our habits of thinking, our expectations of yearly increases in material welfare, our aspirations regarding material welfare of the poor, and an increasing awareness of the resource limitations of our planet are beginning to compel us to recognize that we have to give some hard thought to the problem of conflicting goals with respect to growth. The declining community, of course, has a special interest in the cost of growth. It is not in a position to squander resources in pursuit of inadequately considered options. The risks of poor decisions in these communities probably have more negative consequences than poor decisions in a growth situation.

The problem of absolute and relative economic decline in rural areas presents issues that are both comprehensive and fundamental. It goes beyond the mechanics of identifying and evaluating options facing the declining community. Despite our conviction of the merits of the analytical contribution of our program, we are well aware that the supply of options is partially due to the quality and size of national programs to promote rural development. We seem to have arrived at a consensus that further population growth in major urban and suburban areas is so economically undesirable that a national effort should be made to enable rural areas to stem the tide of migration to metropolitan areas. The assumptions of diseconomies of growth—that is rising marginal costs, public and private, in major metropolitan areas—may be quite sound. But, the decisions of those who migrate to metropolitan areas and those who bring capital to urban areas are based on average cost considerations, not marginal costs. The net migration of population and the flows of capital suggest that the economics of location as perceived by entrepreneurs and the labor force still predominantly favor the major urban and sub-urban areas.

On the other hand, it is likely that some rural communities will decline absolutely and relatively, whatever the size of a national pro-gram of rural development. The pattern of development in Cali-fornia illustrates, in part, this kind of situation. While the economy and population of the state has been expanding at rates above the national average, a study of at least one county indicates that under the best of circumstances a 15–20 percent decline in total economic activity can be expected in a decade.

The outlook is for continued use of input-output models to help people specify economic problems and identify which solutions they want to implement.

Our program evolved slowly, and has been based on a few key county extension people, staff participation (even though some of the physical scientists originally were skeptical about the effort), and con-tinued involvement with county leaders. While our efforts do not show miracles of economic and social opportunity for declining com-munities, they do indicate that more thoughtful consideration of re-source use options is being made at the county level.

CHAPTER TWELVE

OPEN FORUM

Rural Communities Offer Societal Options

Anne Kunze

AMERICA SHOULD be a society that offers people many alternatives and choices and provides considerable individual freedom. Having the choice of how to live and where to live is one of the most important things that we can provide for this society. Although tiny communities and family farms are in a very small minority, they are important because they offer options to kinds of urban life styles. Small communities also produce the kind of children that grow up to be independent thinkers, not submissive, docile, and easily manipulated persons. The human product from our small communities provides a continual refreshment of society. For example, the children who grow up in company towns don't have the same kind of internal strength and creativity and highly developed human potential as those who come from the entrepreneurship kind of society—the small rural town and family farm. Our objective should be a society that creates independent, highly developed children.

There is a critical need today to teach people in small communities how to operate as group dynamics teams, to organize community planning groups, to analyze their problems and establish priorities, and to implement the decisions they adopt. This effort would be expensive and would require constant nurturing and feeding; there would need to be a continual restoring of the groups' vitality.

All the regionalism occurring in this country is lacking on this point. Regionalism provides for a system of powerful people at top levels, but often there is no way to get information from the top-level planners to people of the small community and vice versa. Communi-

ANNE KUNZE is a farmwife, teacher, community leader, and president of United Services Citizen Council, Inc., Alpena, S.D.

ty planning groups could be the means for building communications between the people and the planners.

I believe the extension service should be an advocate of tiny minorities from small communities who do not have the political or economic strength to fight for themselves. Extension should be a friend, not just a neutral observer standing by to watch our small communities decline and die. By providing small communities with more leadership training and organizational assistance in community development processes, the extension service could be a means of revitalizing rural America.

Mass Secondary Data Manipulators

G. Howard Phillips

AS I review literature concerning decision making within the small community, my concern is that rural development researchers have become mass secondary data manipulators. This approach is useful on the national or regional level, but there are still decisions made at the local level and we do not have much research-based information that recognizes this. What are we doing in using the secondary data manipulation approach is measuring input. We are making all our judgments on the basis of what we put into the system for making our decisions rather than on results. For example, it is well known that rural educational systems are inferior to every educational system. This judgment is based on data such as the number of books in the school library, not on whether anybody reads the books. Or it is based on the salary scale of teachers without consideration for differences in the cost of living in different areas. This is the kind of research information we have today; it is input research. Another well-known deduction is that rural people have inferior health. I don't know how we know that except we have determined that rural people live greater distances from hospitals and fewer doctors practice in rural areas. That is why we know they have inferior health. I recently found out that a West Virginia study involved the medical school's *actually* going out and examining people to determine their health status as a basis for making such a judgment!

G. HOWARD PHILLIPS is Professor of Rural Sociology, Ohio State University.

If we are going to get down to determining what "quality of life" really is, then we must improve our research beyond the secondary data stage.

Research on Declining Communities: The Great Void

Jan L. Flora

TO DETERMINE what kind of research is useful for the stable or declining rural community, one must first know the structural context within which the rural community exists. The first part of this section will be devoted to assessing this context. This is inextricably tied in with the role which the USDA-land grant complex has played in explicating this structure and in discovering farming trends in the United States. Secondly, I will discuss the kind of community research for which there is most urgent need.

GROWTH OF CORPORATE AGRICULTURE. Agriculture is integrally related to the rest of the economy. The urban economy has tended toward concentration of ownership and control to an alarming degree. For example, the 200 largest manufacturing corporations in the United States increased their control of manufacturing assets from 47 percent of the total in 1950 to 55 percent in 1965 [3]. In most major areas of production, a handful of companies control 70, 80, or even 90 percent of the production. These companies are not the most efficient units of production nor do they contribute to lower prices for the consumer.

Whether there is a similar trend toward concentration in farming is in dispute. Specifically, is the family farm losing ground to corporate-type farming? The U.S. Department of Agriculture argues that it is not. J. Phillip Campbell [1], undersecretary of agriculture, in testimony before Congress in 1972 on the Family Farm Act stated: "Family farms, those using predominantly family labor, make up about 95 percent of all farms and produce 65 percent of all farm products sold in the United States. Although these percentages have

JAN L. FLORA is Assistant Professor of Sociology and Anthropology, Kansas State University.

fluctuated slightly, they have been substantially the same for the last
30 years, despite the decline in total farm numbers."

Professor Richard Rodefeld [8] of Michigan State carefully
analyzed data from the Agricultural Census (used also by Campbell)
and came up with a different picture. Although the USDA's figures
for the most recent period are substantially correct if one includes
family-sized tenant farms, their assessment of trends is incorrect.[1]
While family-sized farms showed an increase in sales of 7.2 percent
between 1959 and 1964, owner-operated, larger-than-family farms
(those employing principally nonfamily labor) showed an increase
in sales of 23.8 percent and industrial farms (nonowner operated,
larger-than-family farms) showed a growth in sales for the 5-year
period of 73.5 percent—10 times as great as the growth in the sales
of family-sized farms. The industrial-type farms increased their percentage of sales of all farms from 6.7 to 10 percent. In 1964 they
represented 1 percent of farm numbers.

Rodefeld found other errors in Campbell's testimony. One was a
failure to analyze trends *within* the 20-year period Campbell used
(Campbell mistakenly called it a 30-year period), and the other was a
change in the definition of sharecropper operations between 1949 and
1959, making it appear that family farm numbers and sales showed a
relative increase in that decade [8].

Rodefeld also found serious errors in a 1968 study of corporation
farming conducted by the USDA Economic Research Service (reported
in USDA ERS Agricultural Economics Reports Number 209, 156, and
142). He was able to independently determine the numbers and size
of corporations engaged in agriculture in Wisconsin from income tax
forms. He found that 37 percent of the "corporations" enumerated
by USDA should have not been included because they were not incorporated, had no agricultural business (they were hunting and fishing clubs, recreational farms, tree farms, etc.), or were excess multicounty units. Forty-three percent of the corporate farms found by
Rodefeld and his colleagues were not enumerated by the USDA
study [7].

For those farms appearing in both samples, the USDA "underestimated the total number of acres actually owned by 37 percent,
acres rented by 269 percent, number of cattle fed by 80 percent, number of milk cows by 54 percent, number of sows by 37 percent" [7].
Similar figures were obtained in comparing the two entire universes.
Since the same method of data collection was used by the USDA in 46

1. Campbell used 1969; the latest figures available for Rodefeld's method of
calculation were for 1964. Both used the Agricultural Census. The figures on
which Campbell based his statements actually show family farms as generating
62 percent of the sales.

states in addition to Wisconsin, Rodefeld's study calls into serious question the validity of the entire nationwide study.

One more example merits mention. Secretary of Agriculture Earl Butz has said that "Less than 1 percent of our total farms are corporate farms and about six out of seven (86 percent) of those are family corporation farms. They are really family farms" [7].

Butz based this statement on the assumption that all incorporated farms with less than 10 stockholders were family corporations. Rodefeld found that in Wisconsin only 45 percent of the corporation farms with less than 10 stockholders were family farms (i.e., farms in which the majority of the labor was performed by the manager's family), and that 41 percent of all corporations common to the two studies were truly family farms [7].

I cite this information with two ends in mind:

1. It casts serious doubt on the USDA's contention that corporate or nonfamily farming is not a serious threat.

2. It clearly indicates that the USDA, by its nature a political organization, cannot be relied upon as the sole source for objective statistics—at least in this area.[2]

WHERE IS THE LAND GRANT SYSTEM? Correct information on what is happening in rural America is necessary if a "cure" is to be prescribed. The question then arises: Why were the USDA analyses the only ones available prior to Rodefeld's research, and were there not other land grant college researchers who were working on the same questions so that there would have been other more careful studies to compare with the USDA study?

I think there are two principal answers to this question. One is "fear," the other is "brainwashing." The former is suggested by the experience of Rodefeld when he planned to testify before the House Judiciary Committee as to the inaccuracy of the USDA statistics. He was told by two USDA officials that his testimony was "inappropriate," although they were unable in a 2-hour telephone conversation to make any substantive criticisms of his analysis [6].

This behavior on the part of USDA officials is in no way conducive to freedom of academic investigation. The fear of loss of one's job or research monies because one offends the source of funding can be—and is—a powerful detriment to independent critical research. This is true whether the threat is real or imagined. (It should be noted that Professor Rodefeld still has his job.)

2. The nine-volume hearings conducted by Senator Adlai Stevenson's Subcommittee on Migratory Law of the Senate Committee on Labor and Public Welfare, *Farm workers in rural America, 1971–72*, is probably the best single source of information on the status of corporate farming in the U.S.

The second reason is more powerful than the first. We are socialized to believe as academic researchers that controversial subjects are incompatible with solid scientific research. Rather, social science researchers should seek to research controversial topics, for controversy arises only where change may take place. Hence, by engaging in noncontroversial research, we are almost by definition dealing with static phenomena—and research of static phenomena is often biased toward the status quo.

However, it is not enough to seek controversial subjects. I am skeptical of the ability of land grant researchers to fully explore all viable alternatives. We form a rather closed fraternity; the circles we move in include people like us. One would have to delve into the history and power structure of the land grant system to ascertain all the reasons for this provincialism. Suffice it to say that a major factor is our view that scientists do not take sides with respect to social issues of the day. And by not taking sides, we inevitably side with the status quo. Hence, land grant personnel adopt the neutral position of encouraging greater efficiency and accepting the inevitability of the small and medium-sized farmer being pushed off the land. I sometimes wonder what our reaction would be if we were obliged to attend a conference on an upcoming 20 percent cut in experiment station research funds which was run by a bunch of ruddy-faced, overalled farmers whose principal message to us was to cinch up our belts and "adjust."

NEEDED COMMUNITY RESEARCH. Within the context of an economy that is tending toward even greater concentration, and of a farming sector which nationwide is becoming dominated by corporate-type farms, what kind of community research is needed? The question belies the answer. We should be looking at the effects of economic concentration—particularly of corporate-type farming—on rural communities. The most recent and only study in this area that has been done by USDA-land grant complex is the classic study of Arvin and Dinuba, California, by Walter Goldschmidt [2], conducted in the 1940s. Goldschmidt paired the two towns on a number of characteristics such as population size, distance to a larger center, economic base, ethnic composition, and average farm size. They were quite similar on all of the variables but farm size. The average farm size for the hinterland of Arvin was nine times as great as for Dinuba. Dinuba's farms were family farms; Arvin's were chiefly corporate-type farms. Goldschmidt found that Dinuba had more community services and greater retail trade, a higher standard of living and fewer social inequalities, greater civic mindedness and social welfare services, and greater local control of governmental decisions affecting the community [2]. The reason that Goldschmidt's study was the last of its kind is that the study had major implications for the unenforced 160-acre limitation under the Reclamation Act of 1902. Goldschmidt lost his job, and future appropriations bills carried prohibitions against the USDA "conducting cultural surveys" [4].

Goldschmidt's methodology was quite sophisticated. The principal rational criticism of it was that the difference in median age of the two communities may have explained much of the difference in the quality of life in the two communities [4]. But a recent restudy of the two communities using secondary data suggests this was not a valid criticism. The relative difference in the two towns' ages has diminished considerably and the socioeconomic patterns are similar to those in the 1940s. In fact, although Arvin's (the corporate-farm town) economic base has grown more, the population of Dinuba (the small-farm town) has increased more rapidly [5].

There are a number of shortcomings of Goldschmidt's study in terms of its current usefulness. There is a need for additional studies in different cropping areas, areas of different farm structures, different sized communities, and in communities in different locations within an intercommunity network. The advent of the computer and multivariate analysis allows for the use of a combination of secondary data analysis and community surveys which results in information with much greater generalizability than Goldschmidt was able to obtain.

Maybe it will be necessary for someone to tell rural people how to adjust to living in declining communities even after these studies are done. But I think it is also our obligation to tell the people about the structural causes of this decline. Then they can make their own decisions as to whether they should fight, switch, or just stay there and adjust.

A Concern about Community Communications Systems

R. L. Reeder

IF COMMUNITY and rural development depend on establishment and maintenance of communication systems in the rural community, then we need to put more effort into learning how these systems work. By

R. L. REEDER is Extension Specialist for Community Development Publications, Department of Agricultural Information, Purdue University.

way of a tape recorder and personal interviews, I have been trying to find some clues as to the kind of people who establish and maintain these communications systems. This has led to five premises that now form a basis for my listening to people talk about their problems.

INFORMATION EXCHANGE. Communication systems in the rural community consist of people who are in touch with each other because they have some common problems. The information they share has an exchange value, and they are willing to share it because of that value. But the sharing, the two-way communication, encourages new ideas.

Most often I hear about things that got started at a meeting of a midmorning coffee group at a local cafe. It starts as fellowship and coffee, but if the right people are there, it develops into retirement homes, parking lots, or anything else that resourceful people want for their community. Jaycees come up with a rural ambulance service; a Navy League meeting leads to a five-county retraining program for unemployed people; a Fire Department Booster Club starts a summer recreation program; a retirement home results from comments heard at a church board meeting. The resulting projects often had little relation to the original reason for meeting, but two-way communication permitted new ideas.

DISPERSAL. This communication circle then becomes a dispersal medium into other community groups because of the interlocking membership in relevant organizations and committees. Again it is the people who form the broadened communication system because the problem is of common concern. Sometimes it means the establishment of new committees on an ad hoc basis or it may mean the reinvigoration of old groups because of new interest.

COMPETENT PEOPLE. It may seem a commonplace observation if you work in small communities, but a critical communication factor is the kind of key people who become involved. They need to be competent at two-way communication. We know such people are there, but they are a very scarce commodity in most communities. At least they are difficult to find because, like other native life, they tend to have a "protective covering." Federal agencies like to believe these key people are the politicians, and no doubt sometimes they are. My economist friends tell me the key people are the behind-the-scenes decision makers who do not attend meetings but have reports delivered to them. Sometimes no doubt it is true that they can turn projects off or on with a nod of the head, but they are not building communication systems that will persist in the community.

What I try to find is the person who got the group or idea started in the first place. Why was it started? Who kept it going? Who stayed around to keep the communication going and why did he or she do it?

One of the criteria seems to be that they are available and willing to take the time, because most community programs take years to accomplish. Usually this means the older person whose family is out of the babysitting stage and whose personal business is in such condition that his attention can be turned to the wider community. Usually the key people are members of clubs and organizations where communication lines are already established that permit new ideas to be put into the system. They seem to have a quiet confidence about their ability to talk individually with those significant others who have titles and funds. However, I believe the one rare trait that makes them special is their willingness to go beyond their personal interests, beyond the demands of their role or position and work for the good of the community at large. Often this means more than time—it may cost money, customers, and even friends.

PUBLIC OPINION. One of my surprising findings is that no matter how many key people I interviewed, or how important their role in the community, they have a universal regard for public opinion. They believe that development will come when people in the community are ready for it, and no sooner. That is why they set up committees to test feasibility, and that is why many more programs are put on back burners or dropped than are ever put in motion. They have a valuable sense of timing because they have working two-way communication with other people. This role in the community is precious to them, and they know better than to charge ahead with the delusion that they can change public opinion on critical problems. They do not want to win by a split community.

LOCAL NEWSPAPER. Finally, in the small cities and towns where I have listened, I find that the readers of the local newspaper make up an important communication system. Poor as it is in many instances, the local paper is valuable because it is associated with the community and because it is available to the people. More often than any other citizen, the local editor has been pointed out to me as the one who kept a community idea going. Such editors want to be in the middle of community programs, to keep their readers informed and ready to make decisions, but they lack all kinds of resources for doing it. When you are examining alternatives for rural development, I ask that you keep in mind the small businessman known as the local editor whose contribution is being overlooked and whose needs include exactly the kind of help you can give him.

REFERENCES

1. Campbell, J. Phillip. 1972. Statement before U.S. House of Representatives, Committee on the Judiciary. Family farm act. Hearings before the Antitrust Subcommittee, 22–23 March 1972. Serial No. 28. Washington, D.C.: U.S. Government Printing Office.
2. Goldschmidt, Walter R. 1946. Small business and the community: A study in Central Valley of California on effects of scale of farm operations. Report of the Special Committee to Study Problems of American Small Business, U.S. Senate. Washington, D.C.: U.S. Government Printing Office. (Reprinted in U.S. Senate, Select Committee on Small Business. 1968. Corporation farming. Hearings before the Subcommittee on Monopoly. Wahington, D.C.: U.S. Government Printing Office.)
3. Green, Mark J., Moore, Beverly C., Jr., and Wasserstein, Bruce. 1972. *The closed enterprise system.* New York: Bantam Books.
4. Korkendall, Richard S. 1964. Social science in the Central Valley of California: An episode. *Calif. Hist. Soc. Quart.* 43:195–218.
5. LaRose, Bruce L. 1972. Arvin and Dinuba revisited: A new look at community structure and the effects of scale of farm operations. *Farm workers in rural America, 1971–72.* U.S. Senate, Committee on Labor and Public Welfare, appendix hearings, Part 5A. Washington, D.C.: U.S. Government Printing Office. (Reprinted in U.S. House of Representatives, Committee on the Judiciary. 1972. Family farm act. Hearings before the Antitrust Subcommittee, 22–23 March 1972. Serial No. 28. Washington, D.C.: U.S. Government Printing Office.)
6. *NFO Reporter.* 1972. Muzzling effort backfires: Witness riddles USDA corporate farm study. 16(March 1972): 1 ff.
7. Rodefeld, Richard D. 1972. The current status of U.S. corporate farm research. *Farm workers in rural America, 1971–72.* U.S. Senate, Committee on Labor and Public Welfare, appendix to hearings, Part 5A. Washington, D.C.: U.S. Government Printing Office. (Reprinted in U.S. House of Representatives, Committee on the Judiciary. 1972. Family farm act. Hearings before the Antitrust Subcommittee, 22–23 March 1972. Serial No. 28. Washington, D.C.: U.S. Government Printing Office.)
8. ———. 1973. A reassessment of the status and trends in "family" and "corporate" farms in the U.S. society. Paper read at First National Conference on Land Reform, 25–28 April 1973, San Francisco.

INDEX